MARKS
IN
TIME

125 YEARS OF
MARKS & SPENCER

MARKS IN TIME

125 YEARS OF MARKS & SPENCER

HELEN CHISLETT

DESIGN & ART DIRECTION BY
DAVID ROWLEY

WEIDENFELD & NICOLSON

CONTENTS

FOREWORD BY SIR STUART ROSE

A TRULY BRITISH LOVE AFFAIR

It is a humbling thought that the whole of the Marks & Spencer name, brand and retail empire is founded on a pedlar's tray. The company's story began with a poor young immigrant, Michael Marks, peddling goods around the north of England at a penny a time in order to make a living. Michael must have been a remarkable character. Having arrived with no money, no contacts, no prospects and not a word of English, within a few years he had exchanged the tray for a market stall and, later, the market stall for a chain of thriving shops.

But if that were all M&S was about — the ability to make a healthy business profit — this would be a very thin book indeed. In fact the genius of Michael Marks and, in turn, his son Simon was the vision they brought to the British high street. Simon Marks was the Henry Ford of retailing. It is thanks to him that the public were first offered quality goods of a high standard at affordable prices, something that revolutionised not only retailing, but also contributed to the huge social revolution that took place in the early twentieth century. He was the first retailer to cut out the middleman, a move that allowed M&S much greater quality control on products and better values. In addition, he pioneered standards in the textile and food industries which are still the benchmark ones largely used right around the world today. And if that were not enough, he also made the welfare of his staff his responsibility, about eighty years before phrases such as corporate social responsibility became such ubiquitous buzzwords.

I could go on, but that might spoil this book for you. The fact is that M&S is a unique business and all of us who work for it are rightly proud of the heritage and the values that we continue in its name. We have a lot of things to celebrate, both past and present, that many people know little or nothing about. Above all, the story of M&S is a very human one, so you will also find anecdotes here that range from the comic to the tragic, the far-fetched to the frankly fantastic. I hope you enjoy it and that you will join me in wishing this remarkable national treasure a very happy 125th birthday.

HOW IT ALL BEGAN

The story of Marks & Spencer begins with one figure, Michael Marks. As a young man, he fled his home town of Slonim (then in Russian Poland) for a new life in Britain to escape anti-Semitic persecution. It was a precarious new beginning: Michael spoke no English, had no money and knew no trade – nor was he physically strong.

The youngest of five children, he had been brought up by his father, Mordechai, and four siblings, his mother, Rebecca, having died shortly after his birth. Mordechai was a tailor and part-owner of a grain mill. It is not known exactly when Michael was born – his British naturalization papers say 1859, but his wedding certificate implies 1863 or 1864.

By 1884, he had arrived in Leeds, a city of 'muck and brass'. Leeds was a hub of manufacturing industries, most particularly the rapidly developing clothing trade, and it was here that Michael went in search of work. And then fate intervened. He asked a dapper young Yorkshireman for directions to Barran's (a notable Leeds clothier) – Barran's being one of the few words he knew in English. That man was Isaac Dewhirst of I.J. Dewhirst Ltd, a wholesale merchant's. His manager spoke some Yiddish and through him Isaac learnt some of Michael's story and the fact that he had

been a pedlar in Russia. Michael must have been a personable young man, because there and then Isaac offered to lend him £5. Michael asked whether he could use it to buy goods from Dewhirst's warehouse, with the aim of peddling these around the surrounding countryside. Isaac agreed, so becoming the first ever supplier of the business that was to grow into the world famous Marks & Spencer. By happy circumstance, Dewhirst is still an M&S supplier today.

First Steps

Nobody knows for sure where Michael began his peddling, but most likely it was in the area around Stockton-on-Tees. The historian Goronwy Rees once wrote that his stock would have been modest: buttons, mending wools, pins, needles, tapes, tablecloths, woollen socks and stockings – all carefully chosen for people on low incomes whose clothes were largely made at home. With no shop rent and no overheads, it was the ideal way for an ambitious young man to start up in business. Legend has it that, unable to speak English, he attached a sign to his tray that read 'Don't Ask The Price, It's A Penny'. If true, it was certainly an early example of his nose for business. He chose his stock carefully and did well, soon paying back his £5 debt to Isaac.

In fact he did so well that he did not stay in peddling for long. Within months, he had moved up the retail ladder to a stall on the open market in Kirkgate, Leeds, naming it Marks' Penny Bazaar, with the same no-nonsense slogan proudly displayed. It would be fair to say that the first Marks & Spencer premises were a trestle table of 6ft by 4ft. To take advantage of different market days, Michael expanded his business to at least five other towns in the north of England, including Birkenhead, Castleford, Chesterfield, Wakefield and Warrington. However, in 1892 a tragedy put an end to his trading from open markets. In Birkenhead, he engaged a local girl as a sales assistant, but owing to the market's exposed site and the viciously cold weather, she contracted pneumonia and died. Michael was devastated by guilt. From then on, he made the move to covered markets, arcades and eventually to high street shops.

Michael Marks, the founder of Marks & Spencer. By the time this photograph was taken, probably at the turn of the 20th century, Michael had left the itinerant life of a pedlar far behind him and joined the affluent society of Manchester.

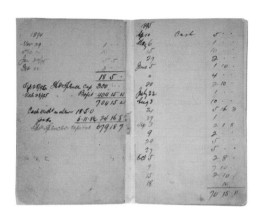

This is the first two pages of Tom Spencer's cash diary. His investment of £300 is shown, as are the profits and values of the company.

Michael's market customers were working-class people on low incomes. He sold anything that might be considered useful and which fitted into his penny (1d) price point. With no need to ask the price and no point in haggling over it, even customers with very little money could shop with ease.

The peak of activity in a city market was Saturday night, by which time most people had received their weekly wages. The introduction of gas lighting meant that market hours could be extended well into the evening, closing time being as late as midnight on Saturdays. Pity the poor sales assistants – some worked up to 90-hour weeks. Michael, always a kindly man, did his best to improve conditions for his own workers, erecting wooden platforms for them to stand on in the market halls, so that their feet would not get so cold. When he later opened Penny Bazaar shops, he provided gas rings so that the girls could heat their lunches and make tea.

Family

Fate intervened again on Michael's behalf when it came to finding a wife. While visiting Stockton-on-Tees on business, he began chatting to a stranger as they both sheltered from a downpour of rain. The stranger, whose name was Cohen and who was also a refugee from Russia, invited Michael home and introduced him to his daughter, Hannah. They fell in love and were married on 19 November 1886, when Hannah was 21 years old. Hannah was an excellent and devoted match for Michael, helping him by working into the night assembling sewing kits and supervising stock. Sadly their first child, a boy, died at birth, but five more children were born to them: Rebecca, Simon (who was born in 1888), Miriam, Matilda and Elaine. Michael grew prosperous enough to move the family first to Wigan and then, in 1894, to Manchester.

That year marked another turning point. By this time, Michael had a dozen or so Penny Bazaar market stalls. He wanted to expand the business, which meant he needed investment – a partner. He first approached his old friend, Isaac Dewhirst,

but Dewhirst declined the chance, instead recommending his chief cashier, Tom Spencer. Tom was a thrifty Yorkshireman, then 42 years old, with a love of cricket and, sadly, drink. He put his life savings of £300 into buying a half-share of Marks' Penny Bazaars and a historic chapter in British retailing began.

In Manchester, Michael and his family lived over the first Marks & Spencer Penny Bazaar shop. Once again, he broke the mould by inviting customers to browse, even having the words 'Admission Free' painted on the fascia to encourage people through the door. The Marks family then moved to a more spacious home at 396 Bury Road – the same street as Simon's new friend, Israel Sieff, who lived at number 408. The first contact between the two families had occurred a few months earlier when Israel Sieff had found himself walking behind three girls dressed in fur-trimmed winter coats. In particular he noticed the pretty legs of the tallest and recalled later: "I wanted to see if she had the kind of face I felt instinctively without instruction should go with the legs." That girl was Rebecca (or Becky) Marks, eldest sister of Simon – and her face did not disappoint. Israel later met her at a children's party and was introduced to Simon when he visited the Marks at home. The two boys hit it off immediately, later attending the Manchester Grammar School together.

There is a rather cheeky saying that Marks & Spencer staff work together, eat together and play together. They certainly marry each other. Not only did Israel eventually marry Becky, but in a neat twist of fate Simon married Israel's sister, Miriam.

Expansion

With the new Marks & Spencer partnership in force, business began to take off. By the end of 1903, there were 36 branches of the Marks & Spencer Penny Bazaar chain, of which 24 were in markets and 12 in shops. That year, Michael and Tom formed a limited company with capital of £30,000. The business expanded so rapidly, quickly becoming a well-known name, that by 1908, there were 60 outlets.

However, there was also turbulence along the way. Tom Spencer had decided on semi-retirement in 1903, drawing on his half of the profits but in effect leaving Michael without a working partner and putting a huge additional strain on him.

Top: Tom Spencer became Michael Marks's partner in 1894. A canny Yorkshireman, he put his life savings of £300 into buying a half-share of the business. Tom died just 11 years later, but his name endures thanks to that shrewd investment.

Below: Rebecca Sieff, elder sister of Simon Marks, who married his best friend and partner, Israel Sieff. Simon married Israel's sister, Miriam.

In 1905, Tom died at the age of 53, his life shortened by a dependency on alcohol. The company name that was to become famous throughout the world was in fact based on a partnership of just 11 years.

On Christmas Eve 1907, Michael took his 19 year-old son, Simon, Tom Spencer junior and a business friend out to lunch, planning to visit the Oldham Street store straight afterwards on his own. Tragically, on his way there, he collapsed in the street. He never regained consciousness and died on New Year's Eve, no doubt hastened to his grave by overwork and a fondness for cigars. Michael had been a great benefactor, always eager to share his wealth, and obituaries paid tribute to his generosity and kindness. 'Pioneer of Penny Bazaars – Death of a Generous Manchester Jew' was the headline above one article, which not only outlined his extraordinary rise from pedlar to successful limited company, but also devoted space to his many philanthropic works.

Simon Marks

To Simon, the loss of his father was devastating. Still in his teens and with virtually no training or experience, he had overnight become the sole supporter of his mother and four sisters. The story of Marks & Spencer nearly ends at that point. Simon was unable to take a director's position until he reached the age of 21. To compound the difficulties, Tom Spencer's executor, one William Chapman, now controlled half the shares on behalf of Tom Spencer junior, who was Simon's age. To protect his own interests, Simon appointed one of Michael's executors, Bernhard Steel, to represent the Marks family's interests until he could himself become a director. It was a rocky moment in the history of Marks & Spencer, a point where it could all too easily have become Chapman & Steel. Fortunately for Simon, the two executors disagreed often. However, they did join forces first in 1909 and then in 1911, proposing to increase the share capital to £100,000, knowing that neither the Marks family nor Tom Spencer junior could afford to take up their share. Simon managed to defeat the first such suggestion and relations between Bernhard and William collapsed before the second could be implemented, with Bernhard forced to retire early in 1912.

By 1912, Simon and Tom had both become junior directors and chief buyers under William's chairmanship. This was the perfect opportunity for Simon to develop the entrepreneurial flair he had inherited from his father. In his visits to the Bazaars, he would continually quiz the sales assistants on what was selling and why – then he would visit suppliers and place his orders accordingly. By the eve of the First World War, the 26-year old Simon was director of a successful and prosperous business – but one where he was often in conflict with the Chairman.

William influenced Tom to such an extent that decisions went 2:1 against Simon. There were many boardroom bust-ups, with Simon bringing matters to a head in 1915 by turning up to a board meeting with Alexander Isaacs (an executor of Michael's will) and his old friend Israel Sieff, with the express intention of appointing them as directors. He insisted the poll be taken based on number of shares – which he knew he could win – rather than a show of hands, but William blocked the move, declaring the resolution defeated. Determined to regain control of the company, Simon took the matter to court and won. In August of that year, Simon Marks become Chairman, a move that eventually forced both William and Tom

Simon Marks (left) and Israel Sieff. The two men met as schoolboys, attending Manchester Grammar School together. Israel joined the company as a director after Simon became Chairman in 1916, eventually taking over as Chairman himself following Simon's death in 1964.

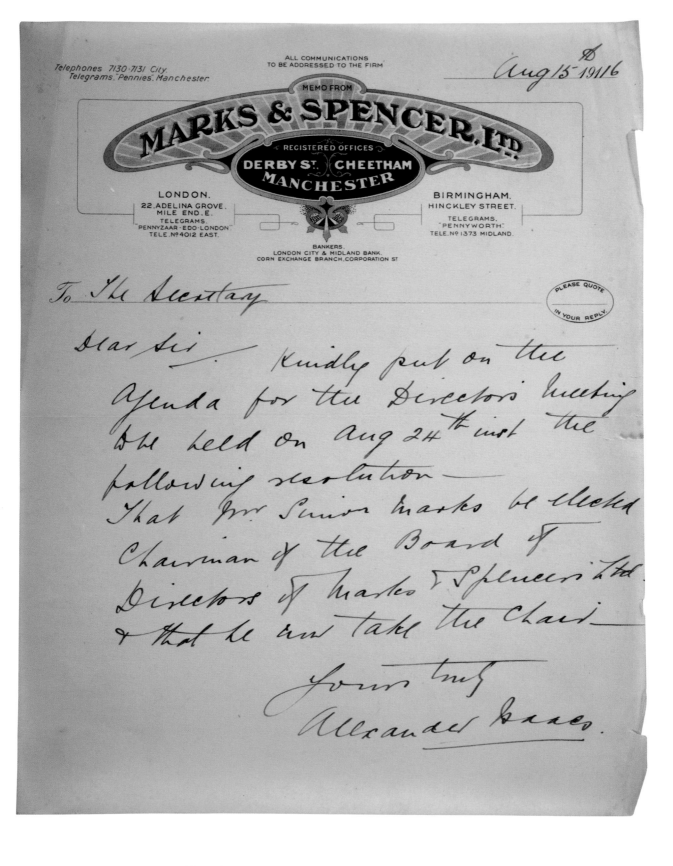

To The Secretary

Dear Sir,

Kindly put on the
Agenda for the Directors' meeting
to be held on Aug 24th inst the
following resolution —
That Mr Simon Marks be elected
Chairman of the Board of
Directors of Marks & Spencers Ltd.
& that he now take the Chair —

Yours truly

Alexander Isaacs.

Spencer to resign in 1917 (the latter died not long afterwards at the young age of 35, a victim of alcoholism as his father had been).

A New Broom

However, in 1917 the First World War was still raging. Simon was conscripted to the Royal Field Artillery in May, just a few weeks after his mother Hannah's death. Gunner Marks, also Chairman of Marks & Spencer, held his board meetings in the Bull & Royal public house close to his barracks in Preston. A few months later he was returned to civilian life, a recognition by the government that he could be more useful to them through his Zionist links. At long last, Simon was free to manage his family firm and take the name of Marks & Spencer to an even greater public, helped in no small part by his old friend, co-director and brother-in-law, Israel Sieff.

After the First World War, Simon began to assess the business in earnest, noting that a growing proportion of the company's profits were being generated in the south of England and that London offered significant opportunities for growth. In 1920, he moved Miriam and his two children, Hannah and Michael, from Manchester to Hampstead in London, and in 1924 the company headquarters also transferred from Manchester to London. In 1931, the head office moved to Baker Street, where it remained for 73 years, first at numbers 72–82 and then – most famously – at Michael House, numbers 47–67.

Such was Simon's ambition that by 1939, Marks & Spencer had 234 stores and 18,500 employees. It was already a nationwide organisation with branches throughout England, Scotland and Wales. If Michael Marks should be remembered as the man who started Marks & Spencer, his son Simon should be equally respected as the man who made it his life's work to grow the company into what it is today. From when he became Chairman in 1916 to when he died – at work – on 8 December 1964, this remarkable and mercurial character oversaw innovation after innovation, transforming not only his own business, but that of virtually every other retailer in the land.

Above: *Simon Marks in later years. A mercurial, ambitious and uncompromising character, he was also a genius of retailing, who transformed the original Penny Bazaars into a nationwide chain of thriving modern stores.*

SHOPPING

One of the fascinations of the story of Marks & Spencer is how it was transformed, under the control of Simon Marks, from a small chain of budget-price market stalls and shops to a landmark of the British high street. Simon ran the company for over 45 years, but it was in the years between the First and Second World Wars that he took his vision of what M&S could be and made it reality. Out went the old Penny Bazaars. In their place came a new generation of large, modern, streamlined stores selling top quality merchandise at accessible prices. Out went reliance on unimaginative wholesalers. In came a new and dynamic relationship with manufacturers that led not only to lower prices, but also to the company's direct involvement with what was made and how it was made. Out went the public's notion of M&S as a place to find something cheap. In its wake came the understanding that quality and value for money were what drove the name of Marks & Spencer forward. But that was not all Simon achieved. At every stage he raised the bar, cementing the name of Marks & Spencer firmly in the British psyche and making it impossible for competitors to ignore the many and various changes that the company introduced to its customers' advantage. If they were to keep up, they had to learn to do business the M&S way.

This chapter is devoted to a few of the milestones that make the M&S story such a unique one, from Simon Marks's radical overhaul of the business in the 1920s to the no less revolutionary Plan A that today addresses some of the challenges of a planet in crisis. The history of M&S is not confined to the company's archive — it is about how a modest family business became an international retailer and in so doing became part of our national identity.

RETAIL
REVOLUTION

This photograph of the Upper Street store in Islington, London, is taken from an album of stores held in the M&S archive, thought to date from around 1910–1920. The flags may indicate the coronation of King George V.

Simon Marks was always a man with a big vision. He wanted Marks & Spencer to be the best shop on the high street, but there were other competitors snapping at his heels, most notably the American-based F.W. Woolworth. In a bid to discover some of his rival's secrets, Simon set off for the USA in February of 1924 on a fact-finding tour. He was not disappointed in what he discovered and later recounted how generous and helpful the American businessmen were whom he met on the trip, commenting *"They seemed to have no secrets from one another – so different from England where everybody seemed to have secrets from everybody else."*

Simon brought back with him some valuable commercial insights: *"I learned the value of more commodious, imposing premises, modern methods of administration and the statistical control of stocks in relation to sales. I learned that new accounting machines could help reduce the time to give the necessary information to hours instead of weeks . . . I learned the value of counter footage: that is, that each counter foot of space had to pay wages, rent and overhead expenses, and earn a profit . . . This meant a much more exhaustive study of the goods we were selling and the needs of the public."*

In other words, he returned fired up with new enthusiasm and optimism, boiling over with ideas that would help reinvigorate business. First on his list was a new pricing structure. The 'Penny Bazaar' title had been gradually dropped in the years leading up to the First World War, owing to rising inflation. By the time of Simon's USA trip, shops were trading under the simplified name of Marks & Spencer, although many of the older premises still had the original fascia boards. Many stores in the US had a one dollar maximum price. In 1927, Simon introduced a five shilling equivalent. This was the first step towards taking the Marks & Spencer brand upmarket, rather than continuing to compete directly with Woolworth's, which sold nothing for

more than sixpence. Simon's plan was to restyle the store into one which offered quality goods at a very competitive price. Secondly, he realised the importance of having much larger stores, where merchandise – in particular clothes – could be better displayed. Thirdly, he introduced a system of sales and stock recording called the Checking List System. This was the detailed compilation of sales information, so that it was possible to track which lines were selling well at which stores. It was a way of both controlling the stock and gauging consumer demand. In fact it was such an efficient method of managing stock that it remained core to the operation

Above: *Simon Marks in his early years as Chairman of Marks & Spencer, a position he held from 1916 until his death in 1964.*

Left: *A newspaper article of 1938 describes the opening of a new Marks & Spencer store in Morecambe. The architects were Messrs Norman Jones and Leonard Rigby of Southport; the building contractor was Bovis.*

THE OLD ORDER CHANGETH, GIVING PLACE TO THE NEW

ON the site of the old Victoria Market in the centre of Morecambe, is now rising a new store for Messrs. Marks Spencer, Ltd., and here is a drawing of what the new building will be like. This sketch shows the eleva fronting Euston Road, and a portion of Market Street on the left. It is expected that the Store will be open June 24th.

The elevations are to be carried out in sand-faced bricks with cream jointing, with reconstructed st dressings and steel windows. They are taking the whole of the site with the exception of a narrow strip Back Crescent. There will be shop windows and show cases fronting Euston Road, Market Street and Victoria Str

The work is being carried out by Messrs. Bovis Ltd., well-known contractors, of London, who have b entrusted with the erection of scores of Messrs. Marks & Spencer's Stores, whilst the architects are Messrs. Norm Jones, F.R.I.B.A., and Leonard Rigby, L.R.I.B.A., of Southport. The structural steelwork has been designed Messrs. S. H. White & Son, of London.

of the company for sixty years — not replaced until the advent of computers in the late 1980s.

The new pricing structure affected the development of Marks & Spencer more than any other decision. Until that point it had sold a jumble of goods — the old Penny Bazaar influence — but the new price limit meant a vast range of goods had to be dropped, because the focus had to be on small profit margins with high sales volumes. Clothing became the leading section of the business — three times larger than any other — and this changed the face not only of Marks & Spencer, but in time of the British high street itself.

EXCHANGE AND REFUND

As St Michael News *stated in 1953, "The customer is always and completely right". On that basis, Marks & Spencer introduced its famous exchange and refund system as early as 1932 when it announced: "Satisfaction is guaranteed either by a refund of money or exchange of articles." It was a no-questions-asked policy, highly unusual in the 1930s and unchanged until 2005 when a time limit for returning goods was introduced for the first time.*

DEALING DIRECT

Opposite top: This image of workers in the Corah factory probably dates from around 1930. Corah was the first manufacturer to agree to deal direct with Marks & Spencer, a move that revolutionised high street retailing.

Opposite below: In 2007-8, M&S developed its first UK eco factory with Westbridge furniture, which produces the entirely 'green' Fern Collection.

Below: This again shows workers in the Corah factory, which is based in Leicester, in the 1930s. Here they are making hosiery items.

G o into a Marks & Spencer store today and it is understood you will only find clothes that carry the M&S label. This is so obvious it hardly seems worth stating, but in fact if it were not for Simon Marks and Israel Sieff, M&S would never have evolved its own ranges – and, quite possibly, no other high street shop would have done so either.

On his return from the USA, one of Simon's goals was to simplify the pricing structure by introducing a five shilling limit. But the flaw in his plan was the fact that Marks & Spencer, like most retailers, bought the bulk of their stock from wholesalers, who in turn bought from manufacturers. To keep prices low and value high, they needed to cut out the middleman. Simon also wanted to create merchandise for the store, rather than be limited to what a wholesaler might have available.

This is where his old friend, and by now colleague, Israel Sieff, proved such an ally. The wholesalers were not going to allow their position to be weakened by permitting a retailer to deal direct with manufacturers. In fact, the powerful Wholesale Textile Association effectively prevented direct trade by blacklisting any manufacturer that dared deal direct. After many unsuccessful attempts at convincing clothing manufacturers to do exactly that, Israel's persistence and diplomacy finally paid off. On his fourth visit to Corah of Leicester, a well-established clothing firm, Isaac persuaded Corah's production director, Cecil Coleman, to take a huge gamble by accepting an order for 1000 dozen men's socks. It was a brave move and one that was even kept secret from Corah's own chairman, who would never have approved it. Indeed Coleman was immediately fired when his boss found out – only to be reinstated when it became clear how Corah's own profits had benefited.

That one sock order effectively changed the face of British retailing. Once Corah realised how much business it stood to gain from Marks & Spencer, it threw its lot in with the company and defied the Wholesale Textile Association. Other

manufacturers soon followed suit. In return for mass-production orders, manufac-turers agreed to charge less per unit and Marks & Spencer was able to pass this saving on to customers through cheaper clothes. It was this that made it finally possible to achieve Simon's vision of high-quality clothing at affordable prices, effectively bringing fashion to the masses.

Overleaf: Lily Cole in her first campaign for Limited Collection, 2008.

Michael Marks once said, "You either make things or you sell them. Don't try both." By deal-ing with manufacturers direct, Marks & Spencer had none of the responsibility for manufacturing, but could become involved in the production process. It meant the company could influence price, quality and, later, design, rather than being presented with goods over which it had no real control. The development of in-house ranges, such as Autograph and per una, would never have been possible without this radical shake-up between M&S and its suppliers.

LIMITED COLLECTION

BUILDING
THE
BRAND

Corah of Leicester was significant to Marks & Spencer for another reason. It had its own trademark, St Margaret, which Simon rather admired. He decided that a similar trademark would give authority to the in-house clothing lines he was now selling: a logo that would be recognised as a guarantee of quality – an important step in rebranding Marks & Spencer from its origins as a successful chain of cut-price market stalls. On 5 November 1928, he 'sanctified' his father by registering the St Michael name under the Trade Marks Act. At first it was applied to a strictly limited range of Marks & Spencer products – shirts, pyjamas, knitwear and macs. Soon it was appearing on a whole range of goods, including garments, toys and – eventually – food. Not that St Michael was the first brand to be introduced by the company: Marspen was an in-house name used for household goods, Marspun for textiles and Welbeck for food. The familiar handwritten style was adopted in the 1950s and is said to be based on the handwriting of the designer's wife, giving it a feminine and friendly appeal. The St Michael logo was eventually dropped in 2000.

Not that this was the first example of branding by the company. The early market stalls and Penny Bazaars carried standard fascias, with Marks & Spencer written in bold red and gold signage. As the chain expanded south, it came into competition with other chains of penny bazaar shops, so carried the slogan 'The Original Penny Bazaar'. Even at this early date, circa 1900, paper bags were printed with the Marks & Spencer name and eye-catching drawings of the head office in Manchester, sometimes with a little prince who gestured towards the company names. A list of all stores was also written on these bags. The ones that survive in the company archive are often beautiful: elegantly illustrated in the 1920s and 1930s, grey with a green logo in the 1950s (the St Michael was now standard) and changing to the more familiar green and gold from the early 1970s.

Staff uniforms were also used to reinforce the brand (see page 204), first introduced in the 1930s, with different ones for textile and food staff. As M&S expanded throughout the country and then the world, its familiar elements were exported with it from signage and store layout to bags, uniform and packaging. Walk into an M&S in Hong Kong today and it will be just as comfortably familiar as one in Norwich or Tunbridge Wells.

The varied logos of Marks & Spencer, including the much loved St Michael trademark, encapsulate the various stages in the company's history. Top left is from a 1930s paper bag; top right from a 1950s annual report; St Michael Registered Trade Mark was the standard used in the 1950s; below this is a 1950s paper bag; to its right is a 1990s logo; at the bottom is the current version introduced in 2004.

MARKS & SPENCER

YOUR M&S

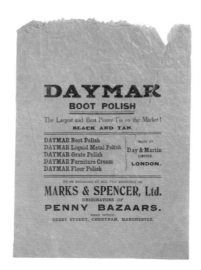

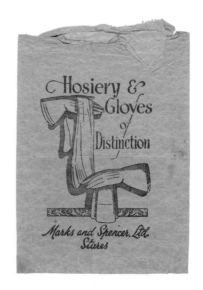

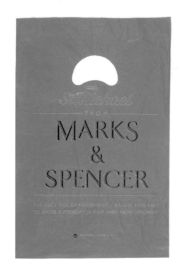

Opposite: *Examples of M&S carrier bags. The earliest (top left) dates from the early 1900s, the most recent (bottom right) is the 5p bag, which raises money for the charity Groundwork. Below are Plan A organic cotton reusable bags, first sold in 2007 as an alternative to plastic bags.*

MYSTERY SHOPPERS

Each M&S store is anonymously visited once a month — twice in the case of the larger flagship stores — by mystery shoppers who evaluate service quality. In 2007/8 that was the equivalent of 6240 visits.

ARCHITECTURE

At the 1939 AGM, Simon Marks spoke these words: "*An M&S store of to-day is in size, equipment and appearance, a very different institution from what it was even as recently as two or three years ago.*"

In the 1920s, after Simon Marks's return from the USA, an in-house department was established to build new stores. Bovis were subcontracted as builders and an in-house architect, Robert Lutyens, son of Sir Edwin Lutyens, was employed to oversee the work and impose a recognisable common design. In the 1930s, the well-known clocks began to appear. The first new 'super stores' opened at Birkenhead and Blackpool in 1923, each with more than double the frontage of previous stores, with plate-glass windows, long, wide counters and greatly improved lighting. A year later the distinctive green and gold fascia – a contrast to the red of Woolworth's – was introduced.

Right: *The original Edgware Road Penny Bazaar opened at no 228 on 1 December 1912, relocating to its current site in 1959. This image probably dates from the late 1910s. The 'Admission Free' sign was to encourage customers to browse.*

Opposite: *The Pantheon store in Oxford Street, London, opened in October 1938. With its radically contemporary art deco architecture, it was hailed as 'London's Finest Variety Store', attracting customers from all income brackets.*

FIT FOR A QUEEN

M&S has enjoyed its fair share of royal visits over the years. The earliest was on 18 March 1932, when HM Queen Mary visited the Marble Arch store (left). The Times *noted the next day that on her half-hour tour, the Queen bought:"an Axminster rug for five shillings, a leather handbag for 1s 11d, a willow-pattern teapot for one shilling and a 21-piece tea service for six shillings". Simon Marks was thrilled to escort the Queen around 'The Arch' himself, noting to a colleague afterwards, "Well, Willie, that wasn't bad for the son of a pedlar!"— but he was also one never to miss a marketing opportunity. Under his canny orders, a junior departmental manager, Eric Lewis, followed the royal entourage at a respectful distance, fixing a ticket on the ranges from which the Queen bought. These read:"As purchased by Her Majesty the Queen". Sure enough, sales of Axminster rugs and willow-pattern tea services leapt skywards following the royal visit.*

During these inter-war years, multiple stores and department stores were increasing rapidly both in size and share of the market. The British high street, although still dominated by independent, local shops, was soon to witness a proliferation of retail names that would become recognisable the length and breadth of the land. The Marks & Spencer store, now looking very different from the old Penny Bazaar, became a feature of every thriving town. It was sometimes next to or opposite Woolworth's – its old rival – and shared the same desire to make its premises look tempting. Frank Woolworth had written after his first visit to England in 1900, *"you are expected to buy, and to have made your choice from the window. They give you an icy stare if you follow the American custom of just going to look around."* The one thing that Woolworth's and Marks & Spencer had in common was to welcome customers positively and never hand out icy stares.

The speed and scale of M&S's expansion at this time is extraordinary. Between 1931 and 1935, 129 Marks & Spencer stores were built or rebuilt. Between 1936 and 1939, a further 33 were added. This could only be achieved by Simon Marks undertaking a massive financial restructuring in order to raise the required

Right: The Basingstoke store in 2004.

Below: The Finsbury Pavement store in London in 2005. Since then, company logos have been rebranded to the simpler and more striking M&S (see opposite).

capital – a risky move that happily paid off. By then, the cost of rebuilding or modernising a store could be as much as £50,000 – compared with £400–500 for opening and equipping a shop in the mid-1920s. In 1930, the company opened its first major store in London's West End on Oxford Street, close to Marble Arch. 'The Arch' as it became known was Simon's personal store, a 10-minute walk from his office at Baker Street. Unfortunately for the staff, he visited every day, interrogating the manager with questions on sales performance, stockholding, new ranges and individual lines – it followed that only the company's fastest-selling and most attractive merchandise was allocated to the store. If something did not please him, he would hurl it to the floor, declaring to the staff around him "You are trying to ruin my business!" Eight years later when the Pantheon store on Oxford Street opened it was hailed as 'London's Finest Variety Store' and, importantly, launched M&S as the upper-income-bracket department store.

In the 1950s, following the devastation wreaked by the Second World War, Marks & Spencer initiated a radical reconstruction and store development programme which was finally finished in 1957. Common design elements were again used to make sure Marks & Spencer stores would be easily recognisable on the high street, but Simon did more than replace what had been there – he transformed the whole chain, giving it "a new look and a new character more in keeping with the specialised goods we are selling".

The 1980s were significant because the very face of shopping began to change, with the appearance first of edge-of-town stores followed by out-of-town sites,

which in turn paved the way for the giant discount stores that have become a feature of British retail. Marks & Spencer's first edge-of-town store was in the 1986 MetroCentre near Gateshead, close to Newcastle upon Tyne. The MetroCentre was seen as a shining example of regeneration in the North East, which ten years previously had been in the throes of recession. Shopping malls have also continued to proliferate. In October 2008, M&S opened its anchor store at Westfield, London, one of the biggest European retail developments this decade.

The flagship M&S at Westfield in west London opened in autumn 2008. Premium finishes, such as ceramic floors and linear lighting, raise customer comfort, but energy-saving systems have also been installed in line with Plan A.

STORE DISPLAY

In 1926, an inventory of store departments in Marks & Spencer included: 'Haberdashery, Hosiery and Drapery, Toilet Requisites, Glass, China and Earthenware, Stationery, Confectionery, Toys and Sports Goods, Fancy Goods, Jewellery, Gramophones, Records and Music, Cutlery, Household Goods, Hardware, Tin and Enamelware, Books and Novels'. In other words, the old Penny Bazaar feel of the shop still lingered. However, the arrival of the five shilling price policy, introduced by Simon Marks in 1927, changed that for ever. The motley selection of goods was edited fiercely in favour of more streamlined departments, which allowed for smaller but more consistent profit margins. By the 1930s, clothing and food (launched in 1931) dominated.

A display of stockings in the Marble Arch store, dating from the first half of the twentieth century. At this stage, windows were usually dedicated to one type of goods only, whether fashion or food.

Marks & Spencer window displays are no longer focused on one single category of goods, but express a lifestyle, combining merchandise from across the store. Seasonal themes link the display with concurrent advertising themes, such as this 'Orient Express' window of 2007. Faux luggage, complete with M&S monograms, adds a touch of wit and echoes the TV advertising story.

As bigger stores were built, attention was also paid to making the interiors as welcoming and inviting as possible. Simon understood the need for lighter, brighter spaces where goods could be displayed to their full advantage. He also increased counter space, making it easier for customers to browse before buying – the Pantheon store on Oxford Street had 1600 feet of counter space.

Display underwent another change when the company expanded during the late 1950s. Until then, shop floors were still of wooden planks which required a monthly oiling – usually on a Saturday night after the store had closed. Fifty-gallon

The Grafton Street store in Dublin, 2008. Exteriors of stores are often designed to complement historic and picturesque settings within towns and cities. The bold green door links to the colouring of the M&S logo.

barrels of industrial oil would be gradually emptied over the gangway areas and worked into the surface by warehousemen and porters dressed in boiler suits and gumboots. Light fittings were mainly opalescent glass shades suspended from the stuccoed ceiling, sometimes with chains well over 10ft in length – if the electricity supply failed, emergency gas lighting supplied a low level of illumination. Heavy mahogany counters and panelling were the standard fittings. As new stores were built and existing ones refurbished, carpet replaced wood, modern lighting was introduced and dark wood discarded in favour of lighter woods and glass.

One feature that Marks & Spencer pioneered from its earliest days was the principle of self-selection. Even the old Penny Bazaars encouraged customers to pick up goods for themselves and examine them before buying, which was highly unusual in the days when items generally had to be paid for before being handed to the customer. Michael Marks had believed in giving people the chance to simply browse if they wished, and Simon too understood that shopping should be a convenient and easy experience. To this day, Marks & Spencer customers are given the freedom to try on items, such as shoes without necessarily having to seek assistance first.

NO SMOKING

In 1959, Marks & Spencer became the first retailer to introduce 'No Smoking' rules. The ban was nothing to do with health, but reflected the company's obsession with fire and safety. However, public reaction was so favourable that it resulted in Questions in the House of Commons when Harold Boardman, Labour MP for Leigh in Lancashire, asked the Minister of Health whether "following the successful introduction of the no-smoking rule into the shops of a leading chain-store company, he would consult with representatives of the retail food trades with a view to possible legislation prohibiting smoking in food stores". The reply was that the Minister "did not think it appropriate to make it a penal offence for customers to do so". Times change.

One of the most far-reaching changes at M&S came in 1948 with the introduction of self-service in the food halls. The first branch to take this radical step was Wood Green in north London. A leaflet was printed for customers explaining the principle: "Please collect all the items you wish to buy in the wire basket provided and take it to the Cashier." It was the first time people could pick things up from the shelves or swap them without having to ask someone behind a counter. Today self-service is of course a feature of every supermarket.

Store innovations and improvements continue to be made. In 2007, M&S launched its first 'eco store' at Bournemouth, a complete refurbishment of one of the oldest stores. As well as more efficient heating, lighting and refrigeration, it incorporates a green roof to capture airborne pollutants, and escalators running at reduced voltage. Other green stores include Silverburn in Pollok, the Simply Food in Galashiels and Westfield in London.

Window displays are also very different today from in Simon Marks's time. Then they were often dedicated to one department, such as hats, knitwear or toys. Today they reflect a total lifestyle with displays that encompass merchandise across the store. They have also become far more theatrical: the flagship store at Westfield in London, for example, features giant 'windowboxes' in mirrored steel with revolving stages for animated displays, complemented by special lighting effects.

Above: At the Westfield store in west London, the Autograph label enjoys a dedicated boutique area, framed by Japanese-style screens.

Overleaf: The store when it was launched in 2008.

ALL
ABROAD

From the 1970s until the end of the 1990s, M&S exploded on the international stage, boasting a retail presence in 683 locations worldwide by 1998, of which 394 were overseas. At the turn of the 21st century, a period of management turmoil led to a reduction in overseas operations. This was not a universally popular decision: Parisians still bemoan the loss of the Boulevard Haussmann branch which opened in 1975 and closed in 2001. Some staff were so disgruntled that they protested first at the Paris store and then at the Baker Street Head Office where they held a rally and presented a petition formally asking M&S to stay. Once Gallic fury had been aired, they then went shopping – most likely at Marble Arch!

Today the M&S international business operates through a network of franchise operations, joint ventures and wholly owned stores, with retail outlets spread throughout central and eastern Europe, the Mediterranean, Middle East, Asia and Indian subcontinent. Hong Kong has long been an important market, while the first flagship store opened in Shanghai in 2008. There are plans to open further stores in the Indian subcontinent and China over the next five years.

The seeds for this international expansion were in fact sown during the Second World War when Israel Sieff was invited by the Board of Trade to go to the USA

with the aim of boosting British exports, which in turn would generate dollars to help finance the war effort. As a result of this, the Marks & Spencer Export Corporation was set up in 1940, eventually providing the Treasury with $10 million from the sale of British textiles and clothing. However, it was not until 1955 that the export trade really developed after an article in *St Michael News* called 'The World Shops At M&S' drew attention to the large number of requests for Marks & Spencer merchandise from abroad. By

"In the 1980s I was a clerical assistant and my role was liaison with our head office in Canada by telex and phone. The employees I worked with out there were desperate to meet me, but company regulations said that my level of job did not entitle me to company travel. In the end, the Canadian team asked Lord Rayner (then Chairman) if I could visit and one November I was allowed to go. Shirley Herman knitted me a hat and scarf so they could recognise me at the airport.

On my return to Baker Street, I was invited to see Lord Rayner and tell him about my visit. I was so worried about what he might ask. When I arrived, there were already a handful of people in the room. Lord Rayner had a glass of Scotch in his hand and he came over and asked, 'How was your trip to Canada?' I was so nervous, I said, 'It was very cold.' 'My dear,' he replied, 'I didn't send you thousands of miles for a weather report.'"

FREDA GRAHAM, RETIRED EMPLOYEE

the mid 1960s, Marks & Spencer was exporting the St Michael brand to over 60 countries. This international enthusiasm was cemented by the fact that foreign custom at 'The Arch' then totalled about 50 per cent of all sales. However, it was not until 1972 that M&S opened its first store abroad – at Brampton, near Toronto in Canada. By then, it had been exporting to Canada for about thirty years.

Selling successfully abroad was a learning curve that continues to this day. Certain garments seem to sell well wherever in the world they are, but size and colour preferences are not so universal. In Hong Kong, smaller sizes are required for petite Asian frames, while in the Middle East dresses and skirts are lengthened. Eastern European markets need winter coats and accessories earlier than in the UK, whereas countries with hot climates require lightweight clothing and flip-flops all year round. The international buying team meets all climatic requirements as well as cultural ones – products are specifically bought for a variety of calendar events around the world, including Eid, Ramadan and Chinese New Year. Interestingly, some of the most popular lines are those associated with 'Britishness' – traditional cashmere sweaters, pure wool skirts, tea and biscuits.

Opposite: The opening of the Shanghai store in 2008 marked a new flagship for M&S in Asia, where there are also a number of stores in Hong Kong. Ranges have been adapted for the new market, including more small sizes in womenswear.

EASY
DOES
IT

Below: *Rugby's Martin Johnson, CBE, is the face of the M&S Direct Big & Tall range. To the right are examples from the Home catalogue, both printed and online, through which most M&S furniture ranges are sold.*

A mantra of Marks & Spencer has long been, 'Giving the customers what they want', although the words 'before they even know it' could well be added. A great deal of the company's success – going right back to its earliest days as a Penny Bazaar market stall – has been founded on the idea that shopping should be pleasurable, convenient and easy. M&S customers have long used their homes as their fitting rooms, so it seemed a natural progression to use them as the shop floor too. In 1998, a mail-order catalogue, Marks & Spencer Direct, was launched and in 1999, online shopping was introduced with a Christmas Gift Shop selling 200 products.

Today M&S Direct includes a home catalogue, flower and wine delivery, Christmas hamper delivery, in-store food ordering service and Lunchtogo, which delivers food and drinks for corporate catering.

The M&S website, marksandspencer.com, was relaunched in 2007 in partnership with Amazon, offering a larger range of M&S products than any of the stores. The website delivers within the UK and to some international destinations. Online exclusive products include Big & Tall menswear, Furniture To Go, Large Appliances, Technology and Made to Measure shirts which allows customers to design their own bespoke shirt. The online wine shop is extremely successful with around 550 wines, including about 20 champagnes.

BAZAAR BUT TRUE!

In the age of online shopping, it is curious to discover that there is still a Marks & Spencer market stall operating in Grainger Market, Newcastle upon Tyne. In 1904, Marks & Spencer acquired two further stalls, trebling its space. The stall still holds its original position and is the last Penny Bazaar still in existence, as well as being the smallest M&S branch.

ADVERTISING

Below: *A beautifully illustrated fold-up leaflet showing Marks & Spencer all-wool swimwear of the 1930s. The M&S archive still holds one of these actual designs. There was also a men's range of knitted swimwear available from the same date.*

So successful have been Marks & Spencer's recent television advertisements, with faces that include Twiggy, Erin O'Connor, Myleene Klass, special guests such as Dame Shirley Bassey and Antonio Banderas, and voice-overs by actors such as David Jason, that many people believe these were the first filmed adverts to be produced by the company. In fact, Marks & Spencer first advertised on television in 1960 and also produced a raft of high-end cinema adverts in the 1950s and 1960s, each one costing around £10,000 to make and often being several minutes in length. Celebrity links are also nothing new. In 1963, the well-known singer Janie Marden sang the words for a Marks and Spencer cinema campaign extolling the virtues of Acrilan. From the 1990s onwards, the company collaborated with famous names, such as Annabelle Croft, who advertised strawberries in 1995.

In fact, Marks & Spencer was advertising back in the early days of the Penny Bazaars, invariably under the famous slogan 'Don't Ask The Price, It's A Penny'. Its advertisement and publication department was set up in 1909 and from then on it made good use of in-house advertising, first in the pages of its *Grand Annual* (1909–1915).

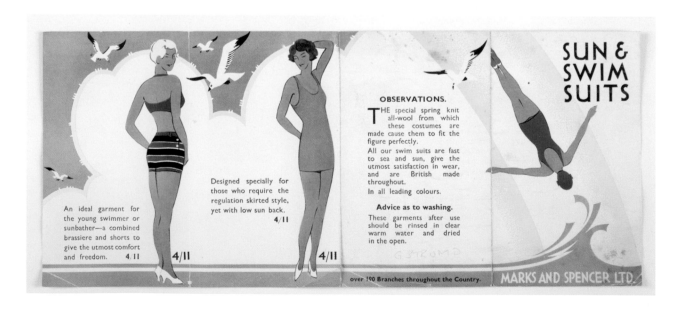

SUN & SWIM SUITS

An ideal garment for the young swimmer or sunbather—a combined brassiere and shorts to give the utmost comfort and freedom.   4/11   4/11

Designed specially for those who require the regulation skirted style, yet with low sun back.   4/11   4/11

OBSERVATIONS.

THE special spring knit all-wool from which these costumes are made cause them to fit the figure perfectly.

All our swim suits are fast to sea and sun, give the utmost satisfaction in wear, and are British made throughout.

In all leading colours.

Advice as to washing.

These garments after use should be rinsed in clear warm water and dried in the open.

over 190 Branches throughout the Country.   MARKS AND SPENCER LTD.

4 DAYS IN TORQUAY

St. Michael News goes 'On Safari' in search of sun and glamour. Off we set with Jean and Helen, Aldine and Frank and a luscious array of St. Michael clothes in crisp Springtime colours. We hired a Dormobile, packed everyone and everything into it. . . . and this is what we found!

A selection of M&S advertising. Top left is a 1950s biscuit advertisement which appeared in St Michael News. To the right of this is a 1970s campaign, also from St Michael News. Below left is Twiggy star-jumping in a 1967 spring–summer fashion supplement; she is wearing a sleeveless knitted shift in Courtelle with crocheted collar and tie belt. To her right is a still from the 2006 Kidswear TV advertisement, which showed children touring London in a yellow bus.

This was followed by *St Michael News*, which launched in 1953, and then *On Your Marks*. From the 1920s to 1940s, it placed advertisements in papers, but usually as part of a new store launch. From the 1950s, it advertised regularly in the pages of women's magazines and newspaper supplements, including *Woman*, *Woman's Own*, the *Daily Mirror* and the *Sunday Times Magazine*. However, it wasn't until 1995 that Marks & Spencer first launched a poster campaign – now it regularly advertises on billboards, bus stops and the Underground, not to forget of course *those* famous TV campaigns, one of which was responsible for a 3000 per cent increase in sales of Melting Middle Chocolate Pudding.

Opposite: *This Doris Day inspired advertisement for the first ever Marks & Spencer Christmas pudding dates from 1958 and would have appeared in the internal publication,* St Michael News.

CANNES CAN

Not only did Marks & Spencer make cinema adverts, it even won awards for doing so. At the 12th International Advertising Film Festival at Cannes in the summer of 1965, a two-minute M&S film Carefree Summer *was awarded second prize against fierce world competition. Made jointly with ICI Fibres and produced by Saward Baker, the film featured St Michael Bri-Nylon summer fashion, photographed against exotic, colourful backgrounds on location in Portugal. It was only beaten into second place by an Italian film,* Seduzione, *which featured the irresistible combination of beer and sex.*

"*My first memory of Marks & Spencer is as a young boy, being taken to the elegant Whitefriargate store in Hull by my parents as a treat, just around the corner from the improbably named Land of Green Ginger Street. It was always a very special place to visit, almost temple-like — and it is incredible that 40 years later I was walking through the doors of Baker Street, this time under very different circumstances.*

During a time when we were searching for ideas to reinvigorate the company's fashion credibility, I recall a chance meeting with Twiggy in the Crown at Southwold. It was a kind of eureka moment! Another was watching the controlled slow-motion explosion of a very decadent Melting Middle Chocolate Pudding in a tiny studio in Camden. It made you want to lick the TV."

STEVEN SHARP, EXECUTIVE DIRECTOR OF MARKETING

The pudding that opened new factories: so instant was the success of the Melting Middle Chocolate Pudding campaign in 2005 that sales increased by over 3000 per cent, making it necessary to increase production accordingly.

PLAN A

Both Michael and Simon Marks believed in the principle of 'enlightened self-interest' – the view that business conducted ethically and altruistically can benefit that business. In addition, trust has always been an important brand value of Marks & Spencer.

In 2006, intense price competition in high street clothing led to a situation in which further price reduction would become ethically unsustainable in terms of factory wages. In order to raise awareness of ethical sourcing and manufacturing issues that contribute to pricing and the hidden 'value' of products, M&S ran a campaign inviting customers to 'Look Behind the Label'. This covered issues as diverse as the management of factory effluent and sustainable sourcing of raw materials, to animal welfare and fair pricing of commodities. Customers began to ask for more information and, in particular, said they trusted M&S to lead the way on helping customers to 'do their bit' on climate change. Out of this, Plan A was born.

Called Plan A "because when it comes to saving the planet there is no Plan B", the plan is now ingrained in every aspect of the way M&S operates: a 21st-century expression of 'enlightened self-interest'.

Plan A in Practice

Here are just a few ways that Plan A has made a difference:

Bags of Good

If you have still not kicked the carrier bag habit, at least you can be sure at M&S that communities across the UK will benefit. Groundwork is a charity that supports communities in need through joint environmental action, helping them to create cleaner, safer and greener neighbourhoods. It has joined forces with M&S to launch a national programme aimed at improving parks, play areas and community gardens. This is funded from the profits from the 5p charge for food carrier bags introduced by M&S in May 2008. In the first seven months alone, this policy raised over £800,000 for the charity and saved an estimated 200 million carrier bags from possibly ending up in landfill – a reduction of over 80 per cent. Over 30 Groundwork charity projects have benefited so far.

Plan A

- *Climate Change* – to make M&S operations in the UK and Republic of Ireland carbon neutral, only using offsetting as a last resort, and helping customers and suppliers to reduce their emissions too.

- *Waste* – to stop sending waste to landfill from M&S UK stores, offices and warehouses; reduce M&S use of non-glass packaging by 25% and carrier bags by 33%; find new ways to recycle and reuse the materials M&S uses.

- *Raw Materials* – to ensure key raw materials come from the most sustainable sources available to M&S.

- *Fair Partner* – to improve the lives of hundreds of thousands of people in the M&S supply chain and M&S local communities.

- *Health* – to help thousands of customers and employees choose a healthier lifestyle.

PLANS PAST

Not that Plan A is Marks & Spencer's first initiative to save energy and prevent waste. Simon Marks was personally responsible for Operation Simplification in 1956. So appalled was he by the overly complicated paperwork used to run the company that he demanded every form be examined and thrown out if it was not necessary. After a few months, the savings amounted to over 500 million clerical entries per year. Invoicing systems were similarly streamlined. As a result, the company was able to scrap 18 million forms, saving 80 tons of paper per year. Savings in overheads were passed on to the customers in the form of lower prices.

On 10 January 1975, Sir Marcus Sieff – then Chairman of Marks & Spencer – wrote a letter to The Times *responding to a leader on 'How can we all save energy?'. He reported that "by adopting sensible measures" the company had reduced its energy consumption by over 15 per cent during 1974 compared with 1973, estimating a saving of £500,000. As well as designing new stores with better insulation, reducing levels of light and making sure refrigerators were maintained at the correct temperature, he also reported that there were now 'Switch It Off' signs above every light switch in the business. That same year, Marks & Spencer launched its 'Save It' campaign, amounting to £8,500,000 of savings to the company by 1979 and winning it a prestigious award from the International Committee of Shopping Centres.*

IF YOU GO DOWN TO THE WOODS . . .

To offset carbon emissions from furniture deliveries, between 2004 – 2009, Marks & Spencer planted new woodland on the College Valley Estate near Wooler in Northumberland – one tree for every 12 furniture deliveries made. More than 50 per cent of trees planted are silver birch, with the remaining varieties a mix of downy birch, ash, rowan, oak and willow. These woodlands are easily accessible to the public and extend to the largest semi-natural woodlands of the Northumberland National Park, beside the well-trodden St Cuthbert's Way.

The Look Behind The Label campaign of 2006 highlighted the ethical and environmental trading practices of Marks & Spencer. Customer support for this led directly to the development of Plan A.

Any Old Clothes?

If you think the time has come to spring-clean your wardrobe, you could benefit yourself, Oxfam and the planet. In January 2008, M&S teamed up with Oxfam to help reduce the one million tonnes of clothing that go into landfill in the UK each year by launching the M&S and Oxfam Clothes Exchange. Customers who take used M&S clothes to Oxfam receive M&S discount vouchers worth £5 to spend on purchases of £35 or more. Everyone's a winner. In just one year, the Exchange raised over a million pounds for Oxfam and reduced the amount of clothing sent to landfill by around 1000 tonnes.

In addition, clothing samples are donated to Shelter and Newlife to be sold in their own shops, so helping to support the charities' programmes.

Slimming Down:

M&S is committed to a total reduction of 25 per cent on all food packaging by

OUT OF THE TSUNAMI

On Boxing Day 2004, a tsunami caused devastation throughout southern Asia. M&S supported vital reconstruction work in Sri Lanka, donating £250,000 to CARE International for the rebuilding of two villages in Galle, on top of the £2 million donated by customers and the £75,000 donated by M&S colleagues. Today Sri Lanka is the home of Marks & Spencer's first fully carbon-neutral 'green' factory, which produces lingerie exclusively for the company. Owned by MAS Intimates, the plant has been designed to reduce carbon emissions and aims to become carbon neutral. Special eco features enable the facility to save about 40 per cent on electricity when compared to a similar scale factory, and to reduce water usage by about 50 per cent. Built on stilts, it has been designed so that the natural contours of the land and drainage patterns can be preserved.

Sri Lanka is also the location of M&S's first Plan A eco factory, upgraded from an existing building, which produces women's and men's casual wear. The Brandix plant reduced its carbon footprint by 50 per cent from before renovation. As well as significant energy savings, it sends no waste to landfill as 100 per cent of waste is recycled or reused. Other 'green' M&S factories are now operating in Sri Lanka, Bangladesh, China and Wales.

2012, as well as using sustainable raw materials where possible. In March 2008, for example, it announced it had reduced the packaging on its Easter range by a weight equivalent to four adult elephants. In addition, M&S was the first big customer to take Closed Loop's recycled food-grade packaging.

Wear That Waste:

Remember those plastic dresses in the 60s? Happily there are no plans to revive them yet, but M&S has now used over 50 million recycled waste plastic bottles to make polyester, which is used in homeware and bedding as well as in polyester garments (see Uniforms page 204) and reusable shopping bags.

Sir Stuart Rose with plastic bottles similar to those recycled into polyester fibre, used for everything from homeware to kidswear. M&S continues to work with suppliers to drive the development of such innovative technological processes.

FASHION

High street fashion is the staple ingredient of most people's wardrobes. There is a variety of styles, colours, sizes and fabrics to suit a huge range of body shapes, tastes and budgets. We take for granted having so much choice of good quality clothing at affordable prices. We also know that designs seen on the catwalk are no longer the exclusive territory of the rich and privileged, because there will be inexpensive interpretations on offer on the high street within a matter of weeks. The 20th century saw fashion transformed from an exclusive world into a fully inclusive one.

But that is not all. The 20th century also heralded a dramatic social revolution, with women often working as well as running a home. Marks & Spencer reflected the changing needs of its female customers, pioneering technological processes to produce fabrics that had easycare qualities, for example — a recognition that many women no longer had the time or the inclination to spend a whole day each week washing and ironing the family's clothes. Mass fashion, as we understand it today, could not have existed without the many innovations pioneered by Marks & Spencer. These influenced everything from the development of synthetic fabrics and standardisation of colours to the fit, feel and look of the clothes on offer.

In fact, it is not overstating the case to say that Marks & Spencer really invented the whole concept of high street fashion. So radical and far-reaching were the changes it introduced that it has influenced our shopping habits, the clothes we wear, and the quality and performance we expect from those clothes even if we have never bought one item of clothing from any of its stores.

BRAVE
NEW
WORLD

Opposite: In 1957, the Marks & Spencer research laboratory conducted its first size survey, A Scientific Approach to Stocking Sizes. The survey, based on 600 women, led to a range of 'super-fit tailored' nylons going into production.

Both Simon and Israel were determined not to see themselves as 'mere shop-keepers', but to keep abreast of new scientific developments that could benefit the company and its customers. In 1935, Simon installed the company's first textile laboratory at the Baker Street headquarters – a highly unusual step. It was a source of great pride to both Simon and Israel that the company not only sold clothes, but also acted as production engineer, chemist and laboratory technician. The establishment of the laboratory not only allowed poor quality to be understood and rectified, but also enabled M&S technologists over the years to build up a unique relationship with suppliers, setting high standards from fibre to finished garment. This in turn led to the company being first to market with a number of new, high quality products – innovations for which M&S became famous.

Many of the company's pre-war improvements in standards were thanks to a refugee from Hitler's Germany, Dr Eric Kann, a highly gifted industrial scientist and expert in textile technology. Before the Second World War, under his supervision, the textile laboratory concentrated mainly on subjecting fabrics to tests for colour-fastness, durability and shrinkage, all M&S quality standards. Between 1935 and 1939 no fewer than 9000 such tests were carried out. When war was declared, Marks & Spencer technologists cooperated with government scientists in devising specifications for Utility clothing (see page 84), a scheme that drew widely on their own knowledge and experience. One of the consequences of the Utility scheme and of clothes rationing was that customers demanded better quality, hard-wearing garments – something that eventually helped extend good design to the general public. Even before the Second World War ended, Simon Marks was formulating the company's future. In his Annual Review of March 1945, he called for a "*revolution in production and production methods to be achieved by co-operation between scientists, manufacturers and workers*". He also spoke of science producing new raw material processes and the creation of new synthetic fabrics and plastic substances.

It is hard today to realise just how exciting and radical these new synthetics were. Not only did they promise to free women from the tyranny of endless hand-washing and ironing, but they also made it possible to lower prices substantially. As Eric Kann wrote in 1962, "*Man-made fibres have undoubtedly made an enormous*

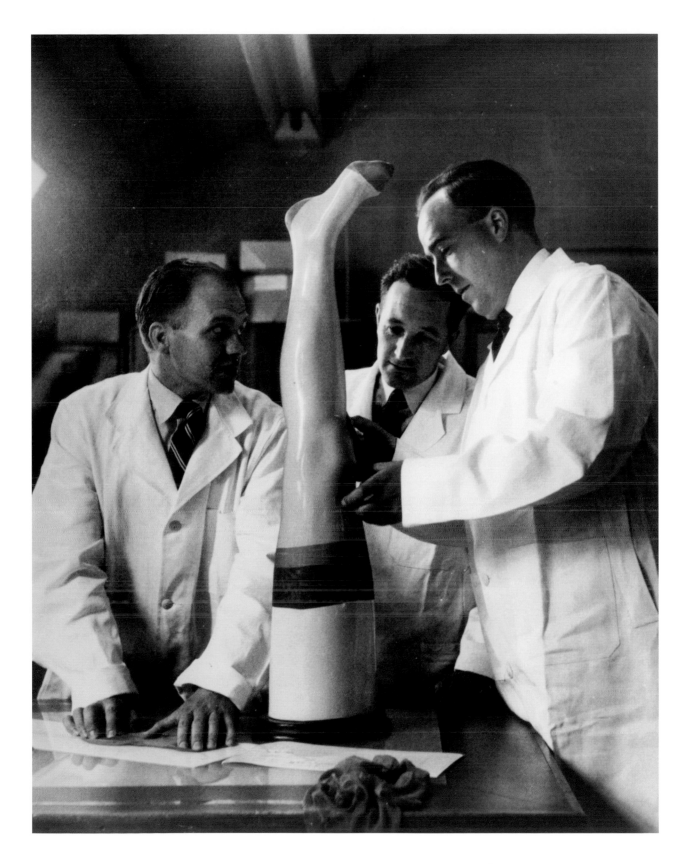

Opposite: *Courtelle was the*
first British acrylic fibre; it was
produced by Courtaulds and
trialled by M&S in 1960,
although this advertisement
dates from the 1970s. Tricel
was a man-made fibre also
marketed by Courtaulds and
sold in M&S from 1957.

contribution to improving the standard of life of millions of men and women, to reducing the burden of household drudgery, and to creating new articles of clothing which meet the needs and tastes of our times."

New Synthetics and Man-made Fibres

One of the fabrics developed for Utility clothing was Utility Schedule 1005, a spun viscose with easycare qualities also known as Marspun. Exclusive to Marks & Spencer, this was used for about 3000 different dresses by the mid 1950s, a vast range that included a huge number of different colour combinations. The hosiery potential for nylon was announced in 1938, but wartime scarcity meant it was not widely available for another decade. By the late 1950s, M&S was selling nylon goods produced by British Nylon Spinners which had introduced its own brand name, Bri-Nylon. Marks & Spencer customers were introduced to polyester – in particular Terylene – in 1960, a fabric that commanded vast world markets because of its 'crease resistant' washable qualities. Two other polyesters, Dacron and Crimplene, were also popular by the mid 1960s. Other 'miracle' fabrics included the acrylic Orlon. All these synthetics were hailed by Simon Marks as "easing the housewife's daily burden".

Today polyester is still used in many parts of the business because of its versatility and durability, for example in school uniforms, blended with cotton in men's shirts or used in fleece dressing gowns to give extra softness. Some plastic bottles can even be recycled into polyester fibre, so it has a 'green' benefit too. Cashmillon is a popular brand of acrylic used today, often blended into knitwear for extra softness. Bri-Nylon, usually known now by its correct name of polyamide, continues to be used extensively in lingerie, swimwear and hosiery. The early 1990s saw the launch of microfibres finer than silk – a new family of synthetics that feel natural, but have easycare benefits.

Easycare Innovations

As well as helping to develop new synthetics, Marks & Spencer also focused on giving natural fabrics easycare qualities. For example, in the 1950s, a resin finish was applied to a cotton used for dresses, so that fabric could be drip-dried with little

ironing necessary. In 1965, it developed drip-dry, minimum-iron cotton poplin shirts. However, one of the most important developments was machine-washable wool. From the early 1950s, all St Michael knitwear had been made shrink-resistant, so that it could easily be washed by hand. In 1972, the company announced its first machine-washable lambswool and Shetland wool garments. In 1995, it launched machine-washable underwired bras. Machine-washable silk and non-iron cotton followed in 1996 – a progression of the company's continuing pursuit of wearable and popular fashion; even M&S silk lingerie is machine-washable. In 2001, M&S launched machine-washable and tumble-dryable wool men's suits, which won it the Queen's Award for Enterprise in Innovation in 2003.

Lycra

In 1986, Marks & Spencer drove the Lycra revolution and in doing so, a new fashion silhouette, first with a new range of hosiery and then with the ubiquitous Lycra leggings which quickly became a runaway best-seller, followed by Lycra bodies. So popular and comfortable was this 'new' fabric that soon it was possible to buy almost anything with Lycra in it, from jeans and swimwear to bedding to shoes. However, Lycra had in fact first been utilised by M&S as far back as

Opposite: The technological advances pioneered by M&S from the 1930s continue today. The Autograph range, for example, frequently utilises machine-washable silk or wool to add practicality to its luxury quality.

1962, when it was added to the girdles which replaced old-fashioned corsets.

In 2008, M&S used enough elastane fibre – the generic name for Lycra – to stretch to the moon and back 300 times.

Colour Standardisation

Not that technological innovation was only concentrated on new fabrics. The Marks & Spencer Colour Bank was established in the mid 1950s, a collection of all the colour samples for different fabrics used in garment ranges – the idea being to make it possible for all buying departments to liaise and avoid unintentional colour clashes on the shop floor. The company also specified standards and tolerances of colour to which all suppliers had to adhere. This meant that the same product could be bought from different locations, but the colour would always match perfectly. Swatches of yarn were sent, for example, to different knitters and dyers, so that a particular shade of, say, red, was achieved irrespective of who the supplier was. Colour standardisation is also a complicated issue because colour is of course affected by light. Some fabrics are more 'metameric' than others – this means they appear to change colour more significantly when the lighting alters. Marks & Spencer was the first retailer to develop a light box in which colours of fabric swatches and garments could be checked, so that they did not suddenly appear to clash when exposed to different lighting. This light box – used from the mid 1960s – could simulate store lighting, daylight, tungsten and ultraviolet.

The early 1980s witnessed a breakthrough in colour matching with the installation of a computer program which could measure and record the precise colour tolerances of a fabric sample. This system – developed by Instrumental Colour Systems (ICS), a British company, and Marks & Spencer made it possible to sell men's suits as separate jackets and trousers – offering different fits – while having exact colour matching. Until that point, a ready-to-wear suit had to be bought as one unit, so men often complained that either the jacket fitted well and the trousers needed altering or vice versa. Colour matching reduced the need for costly alterations. In fact, so significant an achievement was this that ICS and Marks & Spencer were awarded the Queen's Award for Technology in 1984.

IN-HOUSE DESIGN

Below: The New Look was launched in 1947, but continued to be the big fashion story of the 1950s. Marks & Spencer purchased a number of 'models' from Paris couture houses, which were then translated for mass market appeal. This image dates from 1959.

For most people, the world of haute couture is an unattainable dream. But that does not mean to say we are unaffected by the catwalk shows – far from it. We live in an age where we expect designers to interpret fashion trends for us and make them easily accessible through high street shops and the Internet.

Marks & Spencer was at the forefront of this change, its philosophy intent on bringing affordable fashion to its customers. Not only did it play an active role in pioneering new processes and fabrics, which offered customers good quality at inexpensive prices, but it also invested in excellent design, both in-house and through design teams working for suppliers.

A central design department was established within Marks & Spencer as early as 1936, again under the guidance of Dr Eric Kann. The company was determined both to keep abreast of fashion trends and to create a team of in-house experts who could liaise with suppliers. From the very start, Parisian designers were em-

ployed as consultants, an adventurous move for a high street store focused on high volume, ready-to-wear clothing. The 1930s also saw the development of Marks & Spencer's buying departments, with a merchandiser working alongside a selector. The merchandiser negotiated with the supplier on matters of price and quantity. The selector was responsible for the look of a garment and was expected to keep abreast of fashion trends as seen in Paris, Milan and New York.

In the 1950s, Marks & Spencer continued to build contacts with fashion houses, visiting the couture houses in Paris and buying examples – or 'models' – of the latest designs that they could then use as the basis for their own mass-produced equivalent. One of the most successful M&S ranges during this decade was jerseywear, a fashion inspired by the Paris collections. In 1953, jersey garments were available as dresses, cardigans, blouses and skirts. Each garment could be interchanged and coordinated with another. Colours were either classic grey or 'fashionable' cherry, emerald, gold and purple.

Jerseywear enjoyed huge popularity, not only because it was

A design notebook donated to the M&S archive shows lingerie inspiration and sketches for the 1995 collection. By this time, the company was projecting the high fashion image in lingerie for which it has become famed.

fashionable, but because it was smart as well as comfortable – ideal for those with a modest wardrobe who wanted a few well-chosen pieces that could be variously coordinated with each other. In other words, jerseywear was not just about a look, but about a lifestyle – a key development in the M&S fashion story. Paris-based designer Anny Blatt worked on both knitwear and jerseywear ranges as a consultant, injecting the garments with a fashion 'edge'. Her influence on Marks & Spencer womenswear was considerable – not only did the company buy hundreds of 'models' from her in the early 1950s, but she was paid to come over for regular 5-day visits in order to advise on styling, colours and materials. She was also employed as one of the first fashion forecasters, giving presentations to the company on 'forward colour and fabric trends'.

Print Design was one arm of the design department, the creative epicentre of Head Office, where designs inspired from the fashion shows would be sketched out and then painted in various colour combinations, before being sent to manufacturers who would then produce a trial sample. Four to six colourways would usually be finally approved. Print Design worked closely with the Buying department, analysing public tastes both in M&S stores and in fashion centres throughout the world.

In the 1980s, the design department evolved into a consultancy service, liaising with suppliers and providing a seasonal brief for ladieswear, childrenswear, menswear and lingerie. However, in the 1990s there was another shift and the company became more forward with its own ideas. One of its signature looks was 'classic with a twist' – timeless designs injected with a strong fashion element. Examples included a woman's double-breasted blazer in pure wool and polo shirts for men.

Today, the design department is the creative driving force behind the M&S brands as well as those areas for which M&S has long been rightly famous, such as men and women's tailoring, which lie right at the centre of the company's fashion heritage. The team includes garment designers, knitwear designers, print designers, textile specialists and colourists, working across all ranges including womenswear, menswear, lingerie and footwear/accessories. The introduction of a fast-track process four years ago means that catwalk styles, colours and trends can be in-store within as little as six to eight weeks.

Print Design

As well as forecasting trends and developing fashion lines, Print Design also employed significant freelance and in-house talent over the years, particularly when it came to creating its own ranges of fabrics.

Kathleen Guthrie (1905–1981) was a painter and illustrator of children's books. She worked in oil and watercolour, was a silkscreen printer, mural painter and textile designer. The M&S archive contains a spectacular portfolio of work that she produced for the company, most probably in the period immediately before and after the Second World War, some of which we are delighted to show here. Kathleen married the artist Robin Guthrie in 1927 and then the Constructivist painter Cecil Stephenson in 1941, after which she became associated with the avant-garde of Hampstead.

A selection of work for M&S by Kathleen Guthrie. The wax-resistance print, top left, is entitled 'Almond Flower'; the others on this page have no names but are hand-painted onto coloured papers. Opposite is 'Sea-gulls', also painted by hand.

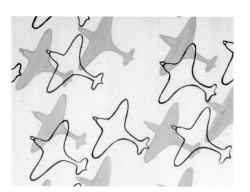

The Embroidery Department

In the late 1960s, the design department numbered over a hundred designers and machinists. There was also one embroiderer employed, her role being to create embroidered motifs for garments that ranged from men's ties and ladies' slippers to children's dressing gowns and baby vests. The work shown here is that of Margaret Nash, who worked for M&S from 1969 to 1974, having studied art first at St Albans and then at Goldsmiths. She worked on designs for 21 departments, including ladies' blouses, ladies' skirts, ladies' dresses, lingerie, swimwear, menswear and childrenswear. It was also her job to liaise with embroidery companies both in the UK and Switzerland once her motifs went into production. Cost was an important factor of her work – if one of her designs was approved by a selector, but came in at too high a price, it was Margaret who had to calculate how best to bring it within the budget – usually by either cutting stitches or dropping a colour.

This is a small selection of work that she produced for M&S during this time, ranging from design sheets to embroidery samples and garments. Most of the work shown was produced for the childrenswear department and features cheeky animated animals or pretty stitching for girls' dresses. Her own favourites were a monkey hanging from a tree holding a lollipop, and an ice-skating rabbit: "I always felt when you designed for children that there should be a little bit of humour attached."

Bottom: a few of the sample hand-embroidered motifs produced by Margaret Nash in 1973, which were then adapted for dress pockets on Junior Miss dresses (see notebook top right).

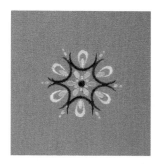

Jan Tricia.
1973. leisure wear.

black cresta
leisure wear dress.
turquoise tie.

T.H. Smith threads
Silver (lurex)
pl. turq. 4638
turq. 4504.

Jan 9th Rosemary Junior Miss
1973. Dress Pockets.

Threads. J.H. Smith.
4221 beige
4413. grey
4348 clover.
4641 red.

Pages from the design notebooks of Margaret Nash, M&S embroiderer from 1969 to 1974. She worked for a total of 21 departments, including childrenswear, lingerie, swimwear and ladies' dresses.

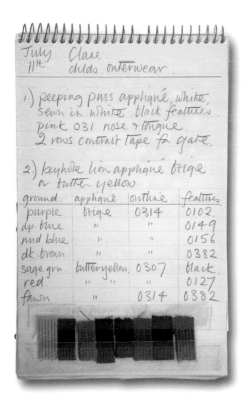

July Clare.
11th childs outerwear

1.) peeping puss appliqué, white,
sewn in white black feathers
pink 031 nose & tongue.
2 rows contrast tape for gate.

2.) keyhole lion appliqué beige
or butter yellow

ground	appliqué	outline	feathers
purple	beige	0314	0102.
dp. blue	"	"	0149
mid blue	"	"	0156
dk. brown	"	"	0382
sage grn	butter yellow	0307	black.
red.	" "	"	0127
fawn.	"	0314	0382

1st June. Penny
Slimmer fit. dresses

brush denim dress. blue
embroi. threads.
4640 salmon.
4427 cream.
4530 green.
543 peach.

67

SIZE
DOES
MATTER

Sizing was one of the biggest challenges for Marks & Spencer when it originally took the decision to concentrate on clothing. Badly fitting clothes had given ready-to-wear ranges a reputation for poor quality, making them a less attractive option when compared to making clothes at home. In fact the whole development of mass-produced clothing rested on a reliable and sophisticated sizing system. From the 1920s, more sophisticated American sizing methods had been adopted by many British companies for this very reason.

Marks & Spencer also took American sizing as the blueprint for its own grading system. In 1957, the M&S research department conducted its first size survey, A Scientific Approach to Stocking Sizes. At this time, stocking size was largely a matter of guesswork, because none of the existing measurement surveys of women had included both leg and foot measurements. The result of the survey, based on 600 women, suggested that six out of ten women bought the wrong-size stockings, so a new range of 'super-fit tailored' nylons went into production. These meant no wrinkling around the ankles and no trouble with seams riding round from back to front.

Until 1988, Marks & Spencer's general sizing for women was based largely upon a survey conducted by the Board of Trade in 1951. But of course the height and shape of women had changed significantly over thirty years, owing to healthier lifestyles. In 1988, a survey was conducted with Loughborough University and the participation of ten Marks & Spencer suppliers. It involved more than 6000 women aged between 17 and 69 at 31 stores. The results, published in 1989, showed that the 'average' British woman was 5ft 4in tall, which was 1 inch taller than 30 years previously. Waist and bust measurements were also filling out.

In 2000, M&S completed its largest size survey of women to date, which involved 2500 women aged from 17 to 70; a separate bra survey was also carried out. This showed the standard dress size had risen from a 12 to a 14, and that the average bra size had increased from a 34B to a 36C. It was followed by fresh size surveys of men and children.

From this size survey, a comprehensive body measurement chart was completed, and using this, 'fit models' are selected to try garments

TEENAGE KICKS

The 1960s fashion for mini-dresses saw skirts get shorter and shorter as the decade progressed. By 1966, the Daily Mirror *fashion pages were suggesting St Michael kilts for 10 year-olds to be worn as mini-kilts by 21-year olds. Vicky Hodge, a model (left), reportedly wore one for children aged three to four. In the late 1970s, staff at Liverpool and Bootle again noted an unprecedented demand for children's tartan skirts. Punk fashion had caused an army of teenage girls to go looking for the smallest skirts they could squeeze themselves into – size 6 was still on the horizon, but age 6 fulfilled the demand perfectly. At the height of the craze, Liverpool sold 70 dozen kilts one Saturday, while Bootle sold an entire season's stock in one week. Not long afterwards, Marks & Spencer also found its menswear cardigans popular with teenagers, thanks in large part to a* Just 17 *fashion shoot, which showed pouting models wrapped up in little else than cardies that could have belonged to their Dads.*

in selected sizes. 'Fit models' are not professional models, but on the contrary are chosen because their bodies reflect those of customers. They don't just try clothes on, but are encouraged to voice their opinions about comfort, movement and style, in addition to how well something fits.

Today, size continues to be one of the biggest challenges faced by the fashion department. Everyone is a different shape, so there are no two size 12s the same. One thing that is interesting to note is that M&S uses a size 12 tailor's dummy as its standard size, rather than the size 10 favoured by most fashion chains.

PLUS
AND
PETITE

*In 1953, Marks & Spencer
launched its first range for the
'shorter woman', based on research which showed that
most women were shorter
than the official average of 5ft
5in. This was the first petite
range on the high street and
was followed four years later
by a range for taller women.*

From its earliest days, M&S prided itself on providing fashion for all incomes, ages and sizes. In the 1950s, it launched its first special ranges for women whose figures did not fit into the 'average' size statistic. In 1953, it announced a new range for the 'shorter woman' – which was defined as under 5ft 2in. A few years later, in 1957, 30 stores sold the 'first-ever' ranges of dresses for women of above-average height (5ft 9in to 5ft 11in). What we today call Plus sizes were available from 1960, when *St Michael News* introduced 'resident head office model Doris Stubbings' under the title 'Big Girl's Fashion Summer' showing clothes for the '40in-hips-and-upwards' contingent. However, it was not until 1987 that Marks & Spencer announced the launch of a dedicated Plus range catering for women up to size 24, later increased to 28, with a Plus range for men introduced the following year. In 2005, M&S launched its Petite collection in sizes 6–18 for women of 5ft 3in and under – the first on the British high street. Particular emphasis was placed on fit and proportion, with careful attention given to arm, leg and body lengths.

Today, many M&S core ranges are offered from sizes 10–24 or from 8–18, depending on what is best suited to a particular garment. Size 6 is a relatively new entry, but one that is particularly relevant in the emerging Asian markets, where women are often size 2 or 4; at present it is mainly reserved for the Limited Collection. Sizes 26 and 28 are available via the online shopping service; men are catered for here with the Big & Tall range.

Plus sizes first made an appearance at M&S in 1960. This window dates from that period – the phrase 'fashions for the fuller figure' on cardigans meant they were suitable for women with a larger than average bust measurement. Today sizes up to 28 are available in selected lines.

LINGERIE

The first M&S lingerie show took place at the Baker Street Head Office in 1947, a welcome diversion after the rigours of wartime. Guests were mainly M&S selectors and department heads, but also included members of the press.

M&S sold its first bra in 1926, one designed to flatten the breasts as required by the then fashionable flapper dresses. Changing trends meant that within a few years it was selling bras with cups that lifted and separated the bust, a look made popular by the 1930s 'sweater' girl. Its main competitor in providing basic ranges of clothing was the Co-op, but what set Marks & Spencer apart was the fact that it sold designs intended to offer a taste of fashion to those on low incomes. In 1938, for example, the company sold glamorous French knickers alongside the far less covetable Directoire knickers, which had elastic just above the knee.

The company noted an increased interest in corsetry after the Second World War. At this time, there were two main types: elasticated 'roll-ons' and more rigid types, fastened down the sides with hooks and eyes. However, by the mid 1950s lingerie had become one of the most fashion-conscious parts of the business and

Left: Nylon nightdresses in evocative shades of flame or aqua were increasingly popular by the mid 1950s because of their easycare qualities. This Lovely Nighties fashion spread dates from the October 1959 edition of St Michael News.

Below: In the 1950s, underwear was designed primarily to give structure. The one on the left was featured in a St Michael News feature offering answers to 'tyre trouble' in 1953. The one on the right dates from the same year.

Marks & Spencer had achieved a 15 per cent slice of the market for bras alone (by the mid 1990s, one in every three bras sold was M&S, a market share the company holds to this day). Vibrant colours were the key to its appeal, with nylon crêpe de Chine nightdresses available in 'exotic' shades of flame, cyclamen, violet, turquoise, aqua and shocking pink.

The trend towards really glamorous and fashionable lingerie began in the 1980s when designs such as the Rose Collection and Feathers paved the way for the high-fashion image that M&S projected in the 1990s.

Recognising how integral lingerie is to the M&S brand, the company has worked with external designers, such as Australian designer Collette Dinnigan (of Wild Hearts fame) and Agent Provocateur (the Salon Rose collection), to produce some really sensational ranges exclusively for the store. This has echoed M&S's collaborations with other leading designers in the fashion department.

For a long time, lingerie choices were split into what is termed 'shapewear' today – the modern version of traditional corsetry – and ranges that were designed to

be beautiful, but which did little to improve a woman's natural shape. The introduction of a new generation of shapewear in 1998 changed all that. In 2001, M&S won the Queen's Award for Innovation for its Secret Support – built-in bra support within sleeveless vests. The highly innovative M&S Magicwear range was introduced in 2003. Today shapewear can be bought that is as glamorous and feminine as the other more overtly sexy ranges. It is also much softer and more comfortable to wear, no longer constructed around sharp wiring and rigid seams.

There is also a huge range of bra types on offer, including low plunge, halter-neck and strapless. If you buy a garment in M&S, you are guaranteed to be able to buy a bra that will complement its cut. Smoothlines, specialist sports, maternity and nursing bras are also available in an array of styles. However, the big story of this century has been knickers as a fashion focus, rather than as a second thought to the bra. In 2008, the most popular style was the boy short – it outsold all other styles by 2:1.

M&S has done more than its fair share to ensure that women wear the correct size bra, with sizes that range from 28AA to 42J. It introduced a fully accredited bra fit programme in 2001, which includes helping mastectomy patients. M&S now boasts 3500 lingerie advisers working nationwide. In 2008, it launched the Post Surgery Range, working closely with Breakthrough Breast Cancer. This features lingerie from existing M&S brands, specially tailored to hold the prosthesis, all available with matching briefs. Ten percent of each sale is donated to Breakthrough Breast Cancer.

Spring 2008 also saw the launch of M&S's Eco lingerie range of vests, knickers and sleepwear – part of its commitment to Plan A (see page 48) – which is made using organic cotton and modal (a fabric fibre made from sustainable timbers). Bras are also produced in the M&S 'green' Sri Lankan factory (see page 52), which has been carbon neutral since day one.

Top left and above:
The 2004 Girls campaign featured Daddy's Girls and Sporty Girls to illustrate the huge range of lingerie M&S offer for every occasion and from 28AA to 44J. Specialist ranges include post-surgery bras.

Noemie Lenoir's exuberance and charm won her a huge following among 'M&S husbands' when she first appeared on the nation's TV screens in the advertising campaign of 2006.

LINGERIE FACTS

* *A third of the UK's female population wears an M&S bra.*

* *Nearly half wear M&S knickers.*

* *The national average bra size is 36C.*

* *M&S sells 45 bras every minute its stores are open.*

* *M&S sells over 50 million pairs of knickers per year, the equivalent of two pairs per second.*

"Even as a child it seems I was destined to go into the lingerie business — courtesy of M&S. Like all the girls in my class my underwear — and first bra — came from there. But while all my schoolfriends were busy making sweet dresses for their dolls, I used to spend hours making knickers and bras for mine, and in the back I would carefully write tiny St Michael labels because I had seen them in my own knickers. The attention to detail stays with me to this day when I am putting together Ann Summers collections — but minus the biro-smudged labels!"

JACQUELINE GOLD, CEO ANN SUMMERS

HOSIERY

Opposite: Although tights continue to dominate the hosiery market, the relaunch of hold-ups marked a revival of interest in stockings. In part, this is because of the continuing enthusiasm for vintage fashions.

The biggest revolution in hosiery was the introduction of nylon – as opposed to more costly silk – in the years after the Second World War. Wartime scarcity meant that nylon stockings did not go on sale in M&S stores until 1947, but their popularity was immediate. No longer did stockings equate with wrinkling around the ankles or seams that rode around the leg. During the first half of the 1950s, Marks & Spencer doubled its market share of nylon stockings from 5 to 10 per cent, selling 15 million pairs by 1954, a fact proclaimed in *St Michael News* under the headline '30 Million Legs Can't Be Wrong'. By 1957, developments in 'seamfree' stockings were announced. In 1963, seamfree 'micromesh' ranges were selling well, with the most popular colour being American tan.

Skirt lengths were also beginning to shorten. Even by 1958, Marks & Spencer's own fashion commentator, Mary Welbeck, had announced: "Women are beginning to reveal inches of leg that haven't seen public admiration since before the New Look." This contributed to the successful trialling of tights by M&S, heralded as 'the best and only way to bridge the mini-gap." Interestingly, they remained fashionable even when skirt lengths became longer once again in the 1970s. Bodysensor opaques were launched in 1997 – their unique microfibre construction designed to 'warm when it's cool and cool when it's warm' won M&S the Queen's Award for Innovation that year.

Today, it is stockings which have made a small but significant resurgence, thanks in part to the technological revolution of hold-ups, and also the trend towards all things vintage. Once a functional buy, Marks & Spencer hosiery is now an important fashion statement, with ranges that include coloured, patterned, opaque, nude, lace and fishnet tights. In 2007, M&S began selling exclusive ladder-resistant sheer hosiery – if a hole forms, they will not ladder. The same year saw the launch of Magic Shaping hosiery, designed to slim hips, flatten stomachs and lift bottoms for a more sculpted silhouette. Indeed, they have been proven to reduce the measurements of 80 per cent of wearers. Luxury ranges include designs in pure cashmere and silk, a return full circle to the days before nylon became synonymous with hosiery.

ACCESSORIES

Accessories have long been an important staple of a woman's wardrobe – a quick and inexpensive way of rejuvenating a favourite outfit. Today, it is a term that encompasses everything from costume jewellery and gloves to bags and shoes. The average pairs of shoes a woman in Britain owns is said to run well into the high double digits, in addition to as many as 35 handbags.

Marks & Spencer has a long tradition of sourcing and selling fashionable accessories, but for years hats dominated that particular market. For the majority of women in the 1950s, hats were integral to a smart appearance, a way of enabling women on limited means to maintain a fashionable look. Spring and Autumn 'Hats Specials' were a regular feature of *St Michael News* in the 1950s, extolling the virtues, for example, of felt hats in exotically named colours such as Pink Romance, Moonlight and Fiesta. Today, hat sales are modest when compared with shoes or – a big fashion story of 2008/9 – gloves, but fascinators are experiencing a renaissance in place of a hat when the wedding season is in full swing. The huge design trend of recent years has been the handbag, driven by interest in designer brands and seasonal 'It' bags.

"It was my Mum who first taught me to sew. She worked in the textile and fashion industry all her working life as a buyer of fabrics. My dad ran a weaving mill, so both my parents were steeped in the word of fashion and product. Marks & Spencer was always part of my life as a child and to this day I wear mainly M&S, although admittedly I like to add my own jewellery. When I was at college studying fashion, it was a pipe dream to work here. It took nearly 30 years for that dream to come true, but it has given me three of my proudest moments. One was the unveiling of the Spring 2006 collection, which was the first to which I could really put my name. The second was the day when M&S fashion went from negative to positive sales — back into the black — which took about 12 months to achieve from when I first joined. The third was becoming the only female executive director on the board of M&S in the Spring of 2008. I was overwhelmed with the support I received, not just within the company but from other female executives of large companies who rang to congratulate me. Sadly my Mum had passed away a few months before, but I know how proud she would have been and how much I owe to her and my dad."

KATE BOSTOCK, EXECUTIVE DIRECTOR OF CLOTHING

"M&S is a series of small hidden surprises for me. Limited Collection is probably my favourite brand and, for me, this is when M&S really sprang back into life. I have an amazing Limited tan goat-suede coat, raw-edge and sprinkled with sequins, which I love and which is about three years old, but I rarely ever go into the Marble Arch store without finding something I love. I think overall, M&S is a bit like a rather loveable, but occasionally 'dotty' aunt who every now and then goes over the top, but you know she would never let you down."

HILARY ALEXANDER, FASHION DIRECTOR, *DAILY TELEGRAPH*

This zebra-print bag was part of the Autograph Spotlight campaign of autumn 2008. Whereas hats dominated the 1950s accessory collections, bags have become the must-have fashion item for today's style-conscious women.

UTILITY CLOTHING

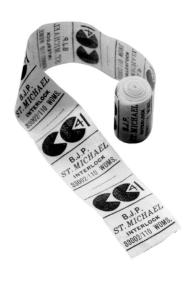

These St Michael Utility labels date from 1941 to about 1950. They appeared on every M&S garment that was sold under the government's Utility clothing scheme.

The Second World War at home was defined by shortages and the need for rationing, not only of food, but of clothes and household goods. June 1941 brought clothes rationing and a coupon system was introduced. This was based on the amount of fabric required to manufacture different types of clothing. The allowance was initially 66 coupons per year, but was later reduced to 48 coupons per year because of shortages.

Before the outbreak of the war, Marks & Spencer's own textile technologists had formulated stringent specifications for basic clothing materials, trimmings and garment manufacture. Many of these specifications were adopted by the government in its Utility clothing scheme – indeed Marks & Spencer technologists co-operated with Board of Trade scientists in devising Utility specifications. This ensured standards could not fall beneath a certain minimum quality, despite scarcity and rising prices. In many ways, the Utility scheme was responsible for improving and extending good design so that it was within reach of the majority.

Utility clothing bore the mark CC41 – Civil Clothing 1941 – basic design in basic fabrics at reduced prices. It accounted for two thirds of the clothes the public could buy, fulfilled government restrictions and requirements, and sold at fixed prices. To conserve material, trimmings and pleatings were restricted, as were skirt lengths and turn-ups on men's trousers. Women used great ingenuity in adding interest and character to this bleak styling: material such as parachute silk, old bedlinen and even black-out curtaining were turned by deft hands into underwear, gloves, scarves and children's clothes. Ladies' stockings – always in short supply – were often replaced with a fake seam drawn down the leg in eyebrow pencil.

One of the benefits of Utility clothing was that it challenged class barriers. Clothes rationing meant that, whatever your level of income, you had a fixed amount of clothes coupons for the year. Of course some people got hold of more coupons than they were entitled to via the 'black market', but many of the old divisions were broken down by the universality of Utility. Clothes by well-known designers were available to all – not just to those in a higher income bracket. To boost Utility designs, the government asked London couturiers to combine in a Utility collection for mass production. In response, fashion houses, such as

Molyneux, Hardy Amies, Digby Morton, Bianca Mosca, Peter Russell and Worth complied with Utility specifications to make coats, suits and dresses, sold anonymously in shops in the spring of 1943. It became unfashionable to look wealthy. 'Fashion' was not so much about looking opulent, as about maintaining a smart appearance with the minimum of effort.

Utility clothes contributed greatly to the turnover of Marks & Spencer during this uncertain period, although many suppliers struggled to meet demand. In a number of ways, the war accelerated scientific and technological progress in the textile and clothing industries. Simon Marks set up a merchandising development department in 1943 to keep abreast of such developments, with a view to the post-war future. After the war, a new textile testing laboratory was opened in 1946, exploring the wonders of nylons, plastics and other synthetic materials. The Utility scheme did not end until 1952, by which time the department had split into three: cloth buying, colour and print, and technology. The application of this new technological knowledge and expertise contributed hugely to better quality merchandise being on offer to the post-war public.

The M&S archive holds a large number of Utility clothes, among them these two dresses and apron. The quality of such clothes was good – M&S's own technologists had helped devise Utility specifications.

THE
NEW
LOOK

The New Look continued to be popular eleven years after Christian Dior first launched it in Paris in 1947. This image of three glamorous women and iconic scooter first appeared in the St Michael News *of February 1958.*

Was it any surprise that after the drab and disciplined Utility, the New Look should cause such waves? On 12 February 1947, Christian Dior – formerly an assistant at Lucien Lelong – reinstated Paris as the undisputed leader of the fashion world with a show at his Avenue Montaigne premises of his Corolle line – the collection that launched the New Look. The signature long and full skirts, lavish with pleats – the more pleats, the more fabric used – were a kickback to the economy and sacrifices of the war. So shocking was the New Look that Sir Stafford Cripps, President of the Board of Trade, was said to have uttered the words, "There should be a law."

By the autumn, the Queen, Princess Margaret and the Duchess of Kent were being given their own sneak preview at the French Embassy. Princess Margaret quickly gave it her seal of approval, while the Queen and Duchess of Kent were soon wearing the below-the-knee length and influencing designers such as Norman Hartnell and Hardy Amies to adopt the style in their own designs.

The fact was that post-war, there was a great desire to get back to normal – and what better way to do this than through clothes? Britain was an almost bankrupt country with national shortages – austerity and rationing dragged on until 1954 in one form or another. The appetite for the New Look was partly nostalgic, a reaction against the rather sexless clothes of wartime and the drudgery of home and work during six difficult and painful years. In just one collection, Christian Dior had outdated everything in the average woman's wardrobe and made her feel self-conscious and drab in a Utility suit. The fashion public were left feeling insecure, particularly about the length of hems. In fact for the first time, the length of a hem was headline news. Television news programmes quizzed

women in the street about what they thought of the new length.

It would have been a massive error of judgement for Marks & Spencer or any other high street retailer to have ignored this national obsession – not least because the New Look actually held sway for nine years (until the death of Dior and the rise of his protégé, Yves Saint Laurent, who caused his own fashion revolution with the A line). The emphasis on a longer, fuller skirt with a nipped-in waist was a huge influence throughout the 1950s – *the* look for the summer of 1956 in Marks & Spencer, for example, was a full cotton skirt worn with a twinset and coloured nylon gloves. In the 1950s, Marks & Spencer purchased a number of 'models' (designs) from Paris couture houses, imported from France under licence. These couture copies were widespread and legitimate design practice – buyers would attend the Paris shows and develop garments back in London, modifying the cut, fit and finish to suit customer and price. Interestingly, those who originated such fashions did not seem to find this a threat, but rather to appreciate the greater prestige and exposure the unashamed copying on the high street gave to them.

In May 1958, Marks & Spencer placed its first colour advertisement In Woman magazine – which would then have been mainly produced in black and white. It too focused on New Look dresses in bold and pretty prints.

CHILDRENSWEAR

Opposite: *Schoolwear has long been an important sector of Marks & Spencer, as this* St Michael News *catalogue of 1969–70 shows. Today, the company offers Kidswear sizes up to age 16, including uniforms.*

Trust is one of the five pillars of the Marks & Spencer brand, so it is no surprise that childrenswear has been an important department within the company since its earliest days. Simon Marks always recognised that M&S was best positioned as a family store, a place where a wife and mother could go to fulfil all her family's needs. Where children were concerned, this did not just mean providing robust daywear, sweet party frocks and baby bonnets, but also schoolwear. Childrenswear is still a department that the fashion team are passionate about, continually looking for ways to improve performance, washability, durability and comfort. One of the most recent innovations is tailored menswear for boys who are still required to dress smartly for school once they are beyond the uniform stage. Having a thriving childrenswear brand also makes it possible for women to shop for themselves and their family under one roof. Most recently, Autograph childrenswear has included sophisticated partywear for girls, smartwear for boys and cashmere babywear.

AS WORN BY ST TRINIAN'S . . .

The Belles of St Trinian's *was made in 1954, starring Alastair Sim, George Cole and Joyce Grenfell, the first film showing the exploits of Ronald Searle's infamous St Trinian's girls. Marks & Spencer provided the film's makers with gym tunics and gym blouses – the authentic apparel for British schoolgirls across the nation. While St Trinian's girls may not have been perfect role models for such uniform,* St Michael News *took the opportunity to remind readers of its quality and ability 'to stand up to hard wear' . . . something that would be required by those devilish school girls.*

Left: *Recognising how important childrenswear is, M&S has invested in excellent photography for a number of years. This action shot dates from 1998, aimed as much at the child as the parent.*

Below: *A selection of Kidswear shots from Spring 2009. M&S produces both playwear and partywear for younger children, as well as fashion-conscious items for older kids.*

"I grew up just outside Norwich and there was an M&S in the town centre, where my mother used to do some of her food shopping. We used to tag along and I remember the staff always being so regimented and consistent in the way they stood, served or spoke to customers. They were always so nice, but aged 9 I used to find it a little tiresome that they were always so cheery and helpful. Then there was school uniform shopping as well, just before going back to school — something every kid disliked because it was a reminder that a new term was about to start, so we would be miserable trying everything on. The best part was food shopping afterwards and trying to smuggle things into the trolley, like prawn-flavoured crisps, steamed sponge puddings, swiss rolls or doughnuts."

TOM AIKENS, CHEF

LUXURY
FOR
ALL

Having championed the easycare synthetic fabrics of the 1950s and 1960s as easing a woman's lot, Marks & Spencer recognised that natural fabrics were enjoying renewed popularity by the 1970s. Denim and cheesecloth, for example, reflected trends made popular by the hippy movement. Wool also enjoyed a renaissance, helped by the 'Cool Wool' initiative promoted by M&S in conjunction with the International Wool Secretariat.

Luxury fabrics were also introduced. In 1974, both men and women's cashmere sweaters were trialled at a few selected stores. Today, more than one cashmere item per minute is sold at the Marble Arch store during peak periods. By the mid 1980s, M&S was selling silk separates, suede and leather, while linen first made an appearance in 1986. That same year, the news that Marks & Spencer was going 'upmarket' was confirmed in an 8-page promotion in the September issue of *Vogue*. Not that the company had any intention of abandoning its traditional customer base – it had built its success on providing good quality and well-designed clothes to people on a moderate incomes, something it continued to do. However, many of its customers appreciated the chance to buy a taste of 'luxury' at an affordable price point. The Autograph label, launched in 2000, used high-end fabrics such as silk, linen and cashmere to emphasise its air of exclusivity. So successful was this that soon such fabrics were appearing regularly in core fashion ranges too.

The late 1980s also saw the company enlisting a new generation of independent, high profile designers to work with it in a consultancy capacity: Paul Smith, Bruce Oldfield and Betty Jackson were among the first big names to take M&S classic ranges and give them a sharp fashion edge. This bridging between the world of high fashion and the high street was one that Marks & Spencer had begun in the 1950s through its link with the top couture houses of Paris. It echoed the company's belief that fashion was not for the wealthy elite, but should be made available to everyone no matter how limited their income.

Today leading fashion designers are still invited to collaborate on special collections, one example being the sell-out collection of Patricia Fields in 2008, famed for the clothes she designed for *Sex and the City*. Most recently, prints launched in collaboration with designer Zandra Rhodes feature in the 2009 collection.

Left: *Myleene Klass wearing Limited Collection in the TV advertisement of 2007. In keeping with its youthful fashion image, selected Limited Collection styles are available in size 6.*

Right: *Erin O'Connor, the face of Autograph, in the Spotlight campaign of 2008. Autograph is an elegant and sophisticated collection, featuring flattering cuts, luxurious fabrics and quality finishing details.*

Overleaf: *Lizzy Jagger in her first campaign for M&S in 2007.*

"Marks & Spencer is like a big family. I count myself privileged to be a part of it. The entire team on the ad department spends the day laughing and enjoying what they do, and I think that is why the campaigns are so successful. People often think the 'famous five' girls live together in one big house and to be honest I love them all dearly and wish that we did!"
MYLEENE KLASS, MODEL

"Landing the M&S contract made me smile. I mean that literally. Coming from the snooty world that is high fashion, I struggled to smile naturally, but with a few professional facial exercises, a grinning girl emerged. She is still grinning to this day!"
ERIN O'CONNOR, MODEL

"We launched per una at 30 branches of M&S on 28th September 2001. After that, I visited every location that wanted to stock it — to see if they had the kind of customers we were targeting. Stores were so keen to get per una that they would put on amazing marketing events to coincide with my arrival, such as a 50-strong Welsh male voice choir at Talbot Green in Cardiff. But my funniest experience was in Neath in Wales, where they had the local rugby team wearing 'we want you, per una' rugby shirts. A woman walked up to me and I thought she was going to tell me that what I was doing was wonderful. Instead she said 'I think per una is overpriced rubbish and you should be ashamed of yourself.' Neath thought she'd ruined their chances of getting per una, but they did. I have nothing but respect for the public — even those who don't approve of what I do!"

GEORGE DAVIES, CREATOR OF PER UNA

"For as long as I can remember Marks & Spencer has been in my consciousness. It was the shop you trusted. Ironically, my Dad, a carpenter from Lancashire, was one of the team in the 1950s who worked on the 'fit-outs' of the new M&S stores in the south. It was also my Mum's favourite shop.

I love being part of the M&S family — the shoots are always so full of fun and laughter. I'm proud to be involved in such a fabulous campaign. Stuart and Steve are a great team and I love working with them."

TWIGGY, MODEL

Left: Portfolio launched in February 2009, featuring Marie Helvin as its first 'face'. Aimed at fashion-conscious women in their 40s or over, the collection features co-ordinated pieces with beautiful detailing.

Right: Twiggy in per una, which was created by George Davies for Marks & Spencer and launched in 2001. The per una brand offers fashionable, Italian-influenced clothes with signature embellishments that appeal to women across the ages.

FASHION & HOME

The M&S collections are not just to do with fashion – they reflect a whole lifestyle, in keeping with customer expectations and aspirations. Autograph Home was launched in 2006, a natural progression from the exclusive Autograph clothing label, with the same focus on style, quality fabrics and a beautiful finish. Inspired by the trend for customers taking short, but indulgent, weekend breaks, Autograph Home replicates a 'boutique hotel style' at home, with muted, neutral palettes, luxurious fabrics, minimalist designs and careful attention to detailing. Furniture, bathroom and bedding is presented as a coordinated look, making it easy to create a sleek and edited interior.

Autograph Home echoes Autograph fashion, offering furniture, fabrics and accessories with a contemporary designer edge, at the core of which are premium materials and quality designs.

MENSWEAR

In its early days, Marks & Spencer provided inexpensive clothes for working-class people, competing with chains such as Lipton's and the Co-operative. Early Checking Lists show the company was selling both female domestic servants' uniforms and men's work dungarees, for example. Even companies that were later to become known for cheap fashion sold at substantially higher prices than did M&S. C&A, for example, was advertising a 'serviceable serge coat' in 1922 at 15s 11d – that was more than three times the highest Marks & Spencer price. No clothing there cost more than five shillings between 1924 and 1939.

Although menswear was a constant from those early days, suits were not introduced until the early 1970s. And, as explained on page 60, it was not possible to sell jackets and trousers separately until colour standardisation had been perfected in the early 1980s.

In a bid to give its menswear a more fashionable image. Marks & Spencer employed the Italian designer Angelo Vittucci as a consultant to the menswear group from 1970. However, it was to be a further twenty years before the company launched its Italian Collection, part of a major overhaul of men's suits, with Marks & Spencer selectors working closely with suppliers in both Britain and Italy on design and tailoring. A number of fabrics used were sourced from Marzotto, a supplier for designers such as Giorgio Armani and Gianfranco Ferre.

Today, menswear features three lifestyle brands – Autograph, Blue Harbour and Collezione – the latter a continuation of luxury Italian style. Innovations in core-product ranges have included water-repellant stormwear jeans, machine-washable suits, crease-resistant linen and cotton shirts, NASA-approved climate-control underwear and fresh-feet socks.

"I met Michael Sacher, an M&S director, about 25 years ago and he said, 'I am fed up with you. We spend so much time in Board meetings talking about what you are doing at Next.' I was very flattered that the gigantic M&S should be interested in what was then a relatively tiny chain of about 100 small shops. I asked what they found so interesting that it took so much time to discuss, and he said, 'Design, dear boy, design.'

What does M&S mean to me? Excellent underpants!"

SIR TERENCE CONRAN, DESIGNER

Above: *Blue Harbour launched in 2002, a collection inspired by East Coast American style and timeless designs.*

Above right: *M&S men's underwear is as successful and popular as the women's ranges — as are the advertising campaigns.*

Right: *Collezione is a label founded on the fabric, cut and flair of Italian fashion, as shown in this 2004 advertisement. Mix and match suits have been one of M&S's greatest innovations, made possible by colour standardisation in the 1980s.*

Take That were the 2008 faces of Autograph menswear.

FASHION
MOMENTS

Above: *This coolly elegant look from 1963 is reminiscent of the 1950s.*

Right: *In contrast, Twiggy featured in a fashion supplement of 1967, her first appearance for Marks & Spencer.*

From the 1950s onwards, Marks & Spencer promoted itself as a fashion brand. Its first such advertisement was placed in *Woman* magazine in 1958, a four-page spread of specially commissioned photography. By 1970, it was also advertising regularly in *Woman's Own* and *Woman & Home*, as well as national newspapers such as the *Sunday Times* and the *Observer*. Seasonal fashion shoots of new collections had become the norm.

The 1980s saw an even bigger investment in high-end photography. In 1982, M&S made its first appearance in *Vogue*, a joint promotion with the International Wool Secretariat. By the early 1990s, it was employing supermodels to cement its image as a fashion brand, a move that it continued to build on from 2005 with its highly successful campaign featuring Twiggy, Erin O'Connor, Lizzy Jagger, Noemie Lenoir, Laura Bailey, Myleene Klass and Lily Cole.

Looking through examples of M&S fashion shoots over six decades, what is fascinating is to see not only the changing styles of clothing, but also how fashion photography itself transformed during this period, from the chic formality of the 50s to the youthful excitement of the 60s; the eccentricities of the 70s to the aspirations of the 80s; the mature confidence of the 90s to the return of fun in the noughties. These are photos that show not just the ebb and flow of fashion, but which act as a barometer for how women's lives altered so dramatically in the second half of the twentieth century.

FASHION SHOWS

From the 1950s, Marks & Spencer staged fashion shows around the country as a way of informing both employees and customers about new products. By the end of the 1950s, it had held more than 35 fashion shows to an audience of about thirty thousand. By the 1970s, these shows were highly organised and were also being used as a way to raise money for charitable causes.

Right: Helena Christiansen exudes confidence and charisma in 2004. The noughties have seen women strengthen their foothold in the workplace, while being equally happy to embrace the role of domestic goddess.

Above: The 1970s saw the emergence of a stronger, sexier woman; this glamorous nightdress featured in the December 1977 issue of St Michael News *and survives in the M&S archive.*

Above right: *in 1996, Yasmin Le Bon epitomised easy glamour in a tight-fitting knitted dress.*

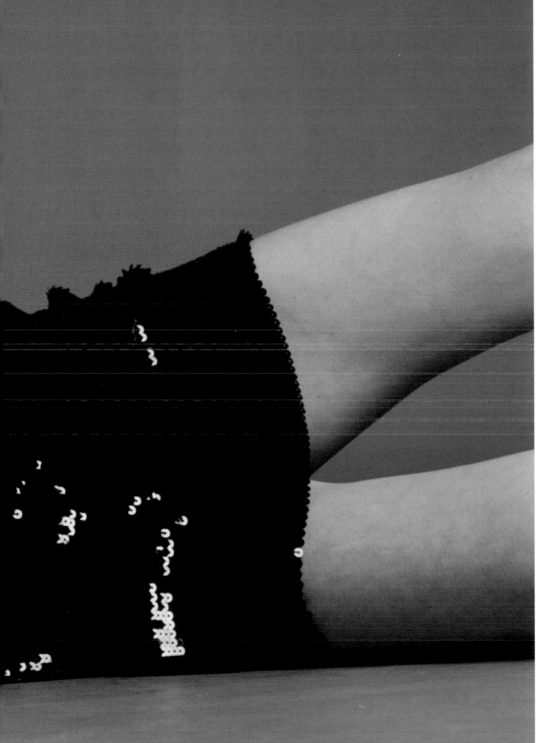

*The 2008 launch of the Sex
and the City collection for
M&S by Patricia Fields caused
huge excitement on the high
street. The one-off collection for
M&S was unashamedly sexy,
striking and show-stopping.*

FACES
OF
M&S

Opposite: Five famous faces – Erin, Myleene, Twiggy, Lily and Noemie pose for the Christmas shoot of 2008. Chosen for their personalities as much as their faces, together they have helped rebrand M&S as a serious fashion force.

It has to be said that of all the many and lovely faces that have graced the Marks & Spencer fashion shoots, the most enduring must be Twiggy, who made her first appearance for the company in 1967, returned in 1995 and then again in 2005. Many other familiar faces have appeared over the years, but not all were famous when they modelled for Marks & Spencer – young actors taking part-time modelling jobs have included Mark Lester (of *Oliver!* and *Black Beauty* fame). It is even rumoured that Roger Moore modelled knitwear back in his pre-Bond days, but sadly the M&S archive holds no evidence of this.

However, even in the 1950s, Marks & Spencer had regular 'faces' to promote its goods. Anne Grierson, for example – a diminutive 5ft 2in – was known best for appearing on showcards advertising M&S oranges, but also modelled everything from jerseywear to appliances.

It was not until 1990 that M&S took the adventurous step of employing models of superstar status to inject further glamour into its ranges. Claudia Schiffer was the first, followed by Linda Evangelista, who was photographed by legendary photographer Patrick Demarchelier in a black miniskirt and black polo-neck – an image that immediately acquired iconic status. Christy Turlington, Amber Valetta and Yasmin Le Bon also made appearances, with the equally superstar male model Eric Osland employed to model menswear ranges. In 2003, Tatjana Patitz made her M&S debut, followed a year later by Helena Christiansen.

In the 1990s, M&S also began to employ sporting heroes, actors, rock stars and media personalities to promote its ranges. Names such as Jamie Theakston, Ian Wright, Jamie Redknapp, Allan Hansen, Bryan Ferry, Jimmy Carr, Bob Mortimer, Martin Freeman and David Beckham all played a role in this stellar line-up. In 2008, Take That became the faces of the Autograph collection.

Most recently, the faces of M&S have included those of Twiggy, Erin O'Connor, Lizzy Jagger, Noemie Lenoir, Laura Bailey and Myleene Klass. Lily Cole was the face of Limited Collection, while Marie Helvin launched the Portfolio brand in 2009.

STAR TURN

When Take That first agreed to appear in M&S advertising, Gary Barlow's Mum told him it was "like being on Parkinson". The roll call of stars who have appeared is impressive — Joan Collins, Graham Norton, Ronnie Barker and David Beckham all appeared pre 2005; Antonio Banderas in 2007. For Christmas 2006, as part of a 'homage' to James Bond, the inimitable Dame Shirley Bassey agreed not only to feature alongside Twiggy, Erin, Noemie, Laura and Lizzy, but also to sing 'Get the Party Started'. Could anything have evoked more glamour and promise of a sparkling Christmas than that? Imagine the excitement behind the scenes as the time came for the star to make her appearance. The finale sequence was rehearsed over and over again using a body double, then cast and crew were informed that the diva herself had arrived and was being shown to the large Winnebago reserved for her own private use. By then the tension was almost tangible . . . the TV production team held its collective breath in anticipation.

As it happens, Dame Shirley was probably holding her breath too. For immediately below her trailer window were eight picturesque reindeer, which appeared to have done nothing more all day than process their food. In fact the whole area was coated in a highly malodorous carpet of reindeer 'slurry'. Would the leading lady pack her bags and leave? Let loose a tantrum of superstar dimensions? Then word came that the Dame had made an urgent and very special request: "More M&S Lavender Room Freshener!" — something apparently she never travels without. And once that was safely delivered, she never batted an immaculately false-eyelashed eyelid. Now that's star quality.

M&S famous faces have included Helena Christiansen (left), Marie Helvin (below) and Lizzy Jagger (bottom right). Lily Cole (bottom left) quickly became established as the face of Limited Collection.

A pregnant and radiant Myleene Klass recreates Ursula Andress's most memorable cinematic moment – as seen in the 1962 James Bond movie Dr No – for a 2007 swimwear shoot for M&S.

Menswear and childrenswear have also enjoyed a creative collaboration with famous faces. David Beckham (above) and Bryan Ferry (left) are among those who have joined the starry line-up.

FOOD

We all have our favourite food indulgences, be it Cornish lobster, English asparagus, Fairtrade chocolate or extra thick custard, but the fact is that M&S has become synonymous with food that is very special indeed. What is interesting is that it nearly stopped selling food altogether, dismayed by the poor post-war quality. Had it not set out to raise standards at every level, from hygiene and quality control to the global sourcing of raw ingredients and tireless quest for new dishes, our lives would have been the poorer, although our waistlines admittedly may have been thinner.

But the M&S food story does not end there. From its earliest days, the company has shown its commitment not only to delicious food, but to good food as well. It championed free-range eggs, embraced organic food, reduced levels of salt, eliminated hydrogenated fats and other 'nasties' from its ranges and took other constructive steps to improve the eating habits and health of its customers. It also takes animal welfare seriously, be it banning crate reared veal or supporting sustainably managed fish stocks. Ethics are high on its list of priorities, as shown by its continuing partnership with Fairtrade and its support for British farmers and other food producers.

The fact is the 'Not Just Food' television ads may set the saliva glands drooling, but they tell only half the story. When you shop at M&S you are guaranteed food that not only tastes delicious, but which encapsulates the five pillars of the company: quality, value, service, innovation and trust.

ALL
WRAPPED
UP

The food department in the Blackpool store in 1938. Self service was not to be introduced for a further ten years, so at this point it operated in the same way as an old-fashioned grocer's, with a wide range of freshly cooked foods on offer.

The Marks & Spencer food department opened in 1931 across all stores, selling fruit, vegetables and canned goods. Windows were often devoted to one perishable item, such as lavish displays of bananas, oranges and grapefruit, at a time when one of the slogans of the day was 'Eat More Fruit'. In 1937, M&S established its own fruit distribution centre in London's Covent Garden market.

Surviving packaging designs from the period are beautifully drawn and coloured – the perfect way to tempt the customer into making a purchase. However, anyone familiar with today's Marks & Spencer food would almost certainly have been disappointed by what lay under the delicious wrapping. In fact own-label M&S food was marketed under the name of Welbeck until the late 1950s, in part because Simon Marks did not think it of sufficient quality to carry the St Michael brand. Quality fell even further during the Second World War, owing to the constraints of rationing, so much so that M&S was on the brink of dropping the sale of food altogether. Then Simon Marks decided to give the department one final chance to bring food in line with the quality synonymous with the M&S name.

This beautiful packaging was designed by in-house designer Charlie Wilkinson in the 1950s. While confectionery was deemed suitable to carry the label of quality, it was not until the mid 1950s that cakes carried the St Michael name.

Above: *More of Charlie Wilkinson's beautifully drawn and coloured designs from the 1950s. Confectionery was a substantial side of the business, while M&S was the first high street retailer to pioneer the eating of grapefruit in the mid 1930s.*

Left and below: Charlie Wilkinson's 1950s designs for fruit jellies, jelly creams and gold label tea. So inviting and evocative are these that some have recently been redrawn and recoloured for M&S food packaging today.

129

Left: The first M&S home-care range was introduced in November 1972, as shown in this image from St Michael News. Marks & Spencer was the first retailer to refuse to stock any brands by other companies.

Below and right: Ready-prepared Chinese dishes were introduced in 1983, nine years after Marks & Spencer's first Indian range was launched. Canned foods continued to be popular, such as this St Michael range of fruit in syrup.

FOOD
FOR
THOUGHT

In the years after the Second World War, key raw materials were still rationed and stretched to the limit – dried eggs, for example, were used in place of fresh. In fact the quality of 'shop cakes' was so low that the public referred to them with derision. It did not help that most were kept on the shelves long after retaining any freshness. M&S had nearly 300 suppliers of cakes, spread throughout the country. The range included slab cakes, pound cakes, swiss rolls, buns, doughnuts and crumpets. Standards of hygiene in the food industry were poor, quality control virtually non-existent and distribution slow and inefficient. The range was limited to the 'non-perishable' variety – i.e. those that would not support the growth of bacteria if contaminated.

Simon Marks gave the food technology team the ultimate challenge: "Develop a range of high quality cakes that we can be proud of and that our customers will buy. If we succeed, the future of foods in the business is assured – but if we fail, the future of foods as a whole may be in doubt."

Sell-by dates were introduced by Marks & Spencer in 1970, but not christened as such until 1972, several years before they became part of government legislation. The chef logo emphasised the freshness of M&S food.

The Technical Executive and Chief Chemist to the Food Division, the first such appointment by any food retailer, was Nathan Goldenberg. Nat was a refugee from the Ukraine, who had been educated in London. Recruited by Simon Marks in 1948, he set about improving quality control, hygiene and safety standards, not only within M&S, but in regard to its suppliers as well.

First, it was agreed to reduce both the range of cakes on offer and the number of suppliers – this would help initiate better quality control. Then the team of technologists set about producing an improved Swiss roll at the M&S bakery laboratory near Paddington, using a newly installed pressure whisk. This produced much better results than any of the suppliers were achieving, improved further by the substitution of frozen whole egg for dried egg and the use of good quality jams by Charles Sheppey. Once the new Welbeck Swiss rolls were put on sale side by side with the previous variety, they sold in greater volumes and faster. Fired up by this success, Nat set about making improvements to every other variety of cake and gateau the company sold.

Freshness was another challenge. Nat pioneered the idea of a 'shelf life' for cakes, so that they should taste as fresh as if they had been baked the day before. For some varieties – such as cream cakes and fruit pies – he insisted on daily deliveries and that they should be sold within the day or destroyed. This was opposed by many store managers, who understandably feared they would lose sales, but in fact the opposite happened. Once the public realised they really were buying 'fresh' at M&S, sales improved noticeably. Later, a 'sell-by' date appeared on wrappers – another Nat innovation that was adopted by other retailers and which eventually became a legal requirement.

So successful was the overhaul of M&S cakes that they were eventually given the St Michael label, a sign that they were of high quality, good value for money, fresh, and produced in clean factories with excellent standards of hygiene and sanitation. They were also sold in clear film packaging, so that the public could see exactly what they were buying.

Above: It was the new, improved Swiss roll that Nat Goldenberg and his team of technologists devised that led to Simon Marks agreeing to continue to sell food. Quality had been so poor that the future of M&S food had been in jeopardy.

Overleaf: A selection of today's delicious mini fruit tartlets.

In 2009, the trend towards a 'home-baked' look led to the introduction of the first M&S cupcakes. The natural colouring and intense flavour of the frosting comes from fresh fruit purée.

CLEAN FOOD AND CLEAN STORES

M&S raised standards of hygiene significantly during the 1950s, particularly in its preparation of food. In 1960, it launched its Clean Food and Clean Stores campaign, which invited 8000 members of the public to visit 'behind the scenes' at M&S to see for themselves the high standards the stores maintained. But that was not all. In the same year, the Nursing Times *published a survey, 'Hygiene in a Store', which focused on Marks & Spencer. In this it stated: "It is strange, and rather shocking, to think that a chain store might be able to teach hospitals anything about hygiene, but it is true that Marks & Spencer recently had a letter from the catering officer of a large hospital saying that he had never seen a fly in their stores and would they please pass on the 'know-how' as he had not succeeded in that battle." It continued: "We all read about the doctor who wrote 'Dirt Is Dangerous' on a ward wall with his finger. He couldn't do that in Marks & Spencer."*

STRAIGHT
TO
SOURCE

In their pursuit of developing truly high-end cakes, the food technologists also began to note the quality of dried fruit used. Suppliers bought in currants and sultanas from Australia, Turkey, mainland Greece, Crete, USA and South Africa. Turkish and Greece produce was best for appearance, texture and taste. However, there was one major disadvantage with their use: many customers complained of 'foreign bodies', such as stones, pieces of wood, glass, metal, thorns, stalks and all kinds of dried vegetable matter. These must somehow have been picked up after the fruit was harvested. It was a huge problem – at the time M&S was using 3000 – 4000 tons of sultanas per year and 700 tons of currants. Nat suggested that he should visit suppliers in Greece and Turkey himself to investigate the problem 'on the spot'. Simon Marks turned the idea down flat – that was until his own grandson broke a tooth on a piece of M&S fruit cake. Permission was granted.

As it turned out, the problem was easy to identify, but more difficult to overcome. Grapes were dried on the ground on wooden trays or pieces of sacking – as they had been for centuries. While drying, they were exposed to the wind blowing in all kinds of other materials. Nat instigated a three-point plan for improvement: drying the fruit in racks raised from the ground; reducing the speed of the machines which washed the fruit, so that more 'efficient hand sorting' could be introduced; and having the eyesight tested of those employed to remove the 'foreign bodies'!

This was one of the first examples of M&S building a personal relationship with suppliers, a way of operating that remains to this day. However, it was in the 1960s that the Marks & Spencer food business began to flourish under the imaginative leadership, first of Marcus Sieff and then later of Michael Sacher and Derek Rayner (both Marcus and Derek eventually became chairmen). The food technologists were one link in an important chain, but of equal significance were the food developers (whose job it was to develop new lines of food), the buyers (who built up relationships with suppliers) and of course the suppliers themselves. Many showed huge commitment to the expansion of the M&S food business, building new factories to fulfil orders and supporting the many new lines and innovations.

The M&S food division had one common goal: to offer the best there was,

whatever that may be. It was the start of a global mission to track down produce of the highest quality, whether it was coconuts from Sri Lanka (then Ceylon), walnuts from France, peanuts from Israel, honeydew melons from Spain or grapefruit from Texas. Air freight played a part in this too. Previously, fruits such as tomatoes were transported by ship from the Canary Islands, so were picked early and expected to ripen during the weeks in transit. The speed of air travel meant that they could be harvested after ripening, vastly improving flavour.

Working directly with suppliers around the world allowed Marks & Spencer to establish the market lead when it came to quality of produce. It revolutionised not only its own-label food brand, but was a huge influence on the way other supermarkets developed. To this day, there are about 100 M&S food specialists employed to source raw ingredients in around 50 countries, guaranteeing that quality, hygiene and, most importantly, taste never deteriorate.

A selection of summer berries, including strawberries, raspberries, cherries and blueberries. By dealing direct with growers, M&S is able to offer customers the freshest and most flavoursome varieties from around the world.

THE
BIG
CHILL

Frozen ready-prepared recipe dishes were first introduced in 1972, including popular staples such as lasagne and fisherman's pie. As the decade progressed, increasingly exotic and global dishes were added to the range.

The easy availability of chilled foods is something most people take for granted today, yet the development of 'cold chain distribution' was something that M&S pioneered in the 1960s, long before other supermarkets realised its potential. What this involved was a nationwide distribution network, which could move dried and chilled foods around the country, both quickly and efficiently. Thermostatically controlled refrigeration vehicles were introduced in 1963, a move that eventually led not only to the easy availability of chilled meats and poultry, but to the top quality menu dishes which became synonymous with the M&S name. 'Cold chain distribution' may not be the most exciting of terms, but what it translated into for those in the food development team was new worlds of possibility.

As with so much pertaining to Marks & Spencer, this radical shake-up began with Simon Marks. In the days before in-store chillers and refrigerated lorries, big retailers such as Marks & Spencer could only offer frozen meat and poultry – fresh was the province of the local butcher. Simon had an intense personal dislike of frozen meat, so Nat Goldenberg and his team were given the opportunity to investigate fresh, chilled chicken. In the late 1950s, they conducted rigorous trials comparing the roasted flesh of fresh, chilled chickens and the frozen variety – each one showed that the fresh bird was both softer in texture and better in flavour. What became clear was that this was largely because of the different ways that fresh and frozen chickens were handled. The first were frozen immediately after killing; the fresh were hung for two to three nights in chillers, resulting in more flavoursome meat.

Fresh, chilled chicken went on sale in newly installed chill cabinets in 1960, an immediate success with customers, who were prepared to pay a premium over frozen poultry for what they perceived, rightly, to be a far superior product. 'Sell-by' dates were later stamped on the wrappers, with instructions either to roast the bird the same day or keep it for no more than two days in a refrigerator.

A boned and stuffed turkey joint, one of Marks & Spencer's most popular dishes. Had it not been for the 'cold chain distribution' revolution of the 1960s, joints and meals like this would never have been available in-store.

Other chilled poultry and meat followed. In 1972, M&S launched its first television commercial (as opposed to cinema ones): 'Remember when chicken used to taste like chicken.'

All M&S chicken today is the Oakham variety, a slower-growing breed that comes from UK farms the company knows and trusts. No chickens are caged and welfare standards are high. The Oakham range includes, fresh, free-range and organic – Oakham chicken is also used in some sandwiches and Gastropub dishes.

LEADING
THE
WAY

Marks & Spencer has always been at the forefront of introducing 'new' foods to the British public. Grapefruit was a virtual unknown in the UK when M&S began selling them in the mid 1930s. Instructions were issued explaining how one should be prepared and eaten, because customers had a natural inclination to eat them like oranges. It is often said that the company sold the first avocados in Britain – while not strictly accurate, it is certainly true that they were almost unheard of when M&S first sold them in 1959. Described correctly as avocado pears, they were put on sale with no instructions as to how they should be eaten. This was a mistake. At least one complaining customer peeled them, removed the stone, stewed them and served them as a dessert with custard. After that the word 'pears' was dropped and a leaflet issued, describing the fruit as a 'salad' and suggesting how it should be prepared and used.

A true Marks & Spencer UK 'first' was the now ubiquitous iceberg lettuce,

A Marks & Spencer food display of fruit dating from the 1930s. Grapefruit had only recently been introduced and instructions had to be printed explaining to customers how they should be prepared and eaten.

introduced in 1980. M&S was also the first big retailer to sell king prawns, con-sidered too risky until a suitable supplier was located in Thailand in the 1970s. One of its biggest successes was popularising smoked salmon, another move made possible through dealing direct with suppliers in places such as Scotland, Ireland and Scandinavia. It wasn't just individual foods that M&S championed, but whole categories: ready-prepared party food, for example, was a 1980s M&S brainchild that is now common to every supermarket.

At times, the company was ahead of the game. Pistachio nuts from Iran were trialled at a few stores in the mid 1960s, but customers knew nothing about them and would often try to eat them with the shells still on. Even when plastic bags were printed giving clear and detailed instructions, sales were poor and they were soon dropped from the M&S range, reintroduced many years later.

More recently, M&S launched the first ever home-grown British purple aspara-gus in 2007, a more tender variety than the usual which can be eaten raw. That year it also introduced 'wonder bean' edamame to its deli side salad – a vegetable which contains all nine essential amino acids, no cholesterol and no sugar.

King prawns have become one of the nation's favourite luxury foods, but M&S was the first big retailer to stock them, having worked directly with producers in Australia, Ecuador, Thailand and, more recently, Honduras and Madagascar.

This cat may well look contented. Food technologist Simon Allison personally samples cat and dog food to ensure that only the best is sold under the M&S name. His own favourite is organic chicken with veg.

THE TASTE MAKERS

One thing that M&S always understood was that attractive packaging was not enough: food had to taste as good as it looked if the public were to be persuaded to buy. Today, there is a huge department of food product developers and food technologists, who specialise in everything from Brussels sprouts to custard, ensuring standards do not fall.

However, the most dedicated tasters must be those who look after pet food – an item that was first sold in M&S in 1970. Senior food technologist Simon Allison samples pet food for the Marks & Spencer luxury range. His favourite is organic chicken with veg – a dish he gives regularly to his three cats, Pants, Socks and Vest. It apparently features 'red flavours' such as heart and liver, with a 'sweeter note' from the carrot. Simon has trained his palate to detect ingredients, such as tripe, which pet owners – as opposed to pets – are known to react badly to. He believes pet food should have the same texture as pâté, but does draw the line at swallowing everything he samples – in case he puts on weight.

READY
TO
GO

Above: *Above: boil-in-the-bag dishes were first introduced in 1974, a radical alternative to frozen or canned meals.*

Right: *This marketing image of 2004 shows mussels in wine sauce, a mouth-watering prepared dish to suit the sophisticated palates of customers today.*

Simon Marks may have had a personal aversion to frozen foods, but by 1973 frozen recipe dishes, such as lasagne, fisherman's pie and pizza were available in 100 M&S stores – a huge hit with the public. There was also a large range available in cans, including chunky chicken, minced beef and curried chicken. Foil-wrapped 'boil in the bag' dishes appeared in 1974, including pasta dishes. Chilled versions followed, the most famous of these being chicken Kiev, which was first launched to an enthusiastic British public in 1979. Marcus Sieff, then chairman of M&S, declared it would never sell in the North with a name like that, but he later recalled, "I couldn't have been more wrong. It sold well everywhere, becoming a multi-million pound business."

The 1970s were like the Wild West for the M&S food division, with buyers and developers as cowboys in search of new frontiers. Buyers were encouraged to source produce from around the world, extending not only the produce sold by M&S but their own cultural and culinary horizons. It was part of their remit to eat the best local dishes they could find and report back on ingredients, cooking methods and regional variations. Food developers were equally well-travelled, working with buyers and suppliers to research dishes and find ways of making them inviting and accessible to the British public. Just as fashion employed expert external consultants, so the food division too benefited from the hands-on involvement of luminaries such as the Roux brothers, Kenneth Lo and Robert Carrier.

From then on, the new ranges pioneered by M&S accurately reflected the public's interest in certain cuisine: in 1974, Indian recipes, such as chicken korma, lamb rogan josh and pork vindaloo were introduced. Chinese dishes, such as spare ribs and egg fried rice were launched in 1983. Chilled vegetable dishes, such as cauliflower cheese, appeared in 1981, while vegetarian main meals and calorie-counted Menu ranges followed in 1985. 1990 saw the introduction of Thai dishes, such as Thai satay and Thai chicken curry in 1990.

Not that innovation has ever stopped. The Gastropub range was launched in 2004, featuring comforting dishes such as cottage pie with cheesy mash and roast chicken with apple wedges and cider and calvados sauce. The additive-free Cook! range was launched a year later, the first such range of pre-prepared food.

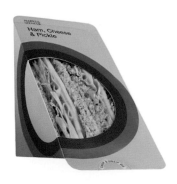

FROM SANDWICHES TO SUSHI

Sandwiches were first sold in 1929 at the M&S ice-cream counters, but it was not until 1980 that they became a key part of the food business – initially trialled in five stores and prepared on site. Sales grew so rapidly that central production was created at three M&S suppliers. The most popular, prawn & mayonnaise, was introduced in 1981 and is still the top-selling flavour. By 1987, there were 25 varieties on offer, available in all stores. In 1994, M&S launched Sandwich Shops in 70 stores, the first high street retailer to include a full ingredients list and nutritional information on labels. In 1999, the two billionth sandwich was sold since the relaunch of 1980. Sandwiches remain the number one choice for those eating 'on the hoof', but wraps and sushi are increasingly popular – both inspired by a food technologist's trip to California. Sushi was first trialled in 1998; today M&S uses enough seaweed to wrap around the M25 every other year.

CAULIFLOWER CHEESE

"I worked in many different product areas over the years, including Fresh Produce. M&S is known for the quality of its produce and only sells Class 1 vegetables, including whole cauliflowers. However, sometimes they are damaged during harvesting, so are floreted instead. Meanwhile we realised that slicing up M&S cheeses into regular blocks produced cheese 'crumbs'. Here were two raw ingredients of the best quality, which could not be sold to the customer in their current form. The answer? Put the cheese supplier in touch with the cauliflower supplier and make a ready meal of cauliflower cheese. A stroke of M&S genius!"
MARTIN HUDSON, RETIRED EMPLOYEE

Eat Well oriental king prawns with edamame beans, sugarsnap peas, red pepper, tatsoi and sweet chilli-and-coriander dressing – oriental dishes are a big influence on the way we eat today.

FLOWER POWER

A gardening department selling items such as flower bulbs and rose trees had been established in M&S as long ago as 1927, only to be dropped as the company became increasingly focused on clothes and food. In 1969, houseplants were trialled in the Leicester store, and in 1973–1975 the horticulture range was extended to include 'bowl arrangements', potted herbs, boxed roses and daffodils. Then in 1979, M&S began trialling the sale of fresh cut flowers at the Pantheon store in Oxford Street. To begin with, there were only four varieties of flower on offer: freesias, carnations, lilies and mixed bunches. Most were sourced via the Dutch flower auctions and transported to England in buckets of water with plantfood – the latter a revolutionary concept – in refrigerated lorries to keep them fresh. The combination of top quality produce sourced direct, chilled transport, speed of delivery and use of plantfood meant that some flowers had a vase life of up to three weeks, a fact which astonished many customers. The trial was so successful that soon other varieties were added to the stock.

As with other departments, external consultants were employed to pass on their expertise. Eminent florist Jane Packer was employed to oversee the introduction of pre-prepared bouquets, many of them using seasonal flowers. Over subsequent years, speciality flowers were also introduced, including cut amaryllis, cut hyacinths, Kenyan red roses and sweet peas. Houseplants were also added to the range, not only the ubiquitous rubber plants and maidenhair ferns, but the sort then usually found only in specialist nurseries, such as 5ft high palms and weeping figs.

Today, it is possible to buy cut flowers at every supermarket and service station, but 30 years ago M&S was the only retailer competing with local florists and nurseries. It was the first time that flowers had been made available to the mass market, on sale at prices that were often well under half the usual quoted.

Today, long-stemmed roses and cascade orchids are sold under the Autograph label within the M&S Flower Shop. Marks & Spencer sell more orchids than any other retailer, but the company also sources as many British flowers as it can, working with growers to extend the season as much as possible. It applies the same ethical standards to sourcing flowers and plants as it does to clothes, homeware and food.

TAKE
A
BREAK

An early ice-cream bar in Marks & Spencer. The Wall's sign pre-dates M&S only selling its own brands of goods. Simon Marks eventually banned the sale of ice-cream because of the mess caused by discarded wrappers.

The first food that could be eaten in-store at Marks & Spencer was ice-cream in 1927 – eventually banned by Simon Marks because of the mess it caused. A few locally organised café bars were also in existence by this time – the Doncaster branch, for example, sold sandwiches, pastries and hot drinks. Then in 1935 and 1936, the first organised café bars were opened in the Leeds, Bradford and Marble Arch stores. Customers could order joints, chops, steaks, fish and chips and other 'popular' menus. By 1938, there were 21 such catering installations. Café bars were not standard in design: some served only teas, while others offered light meals. A large unit would require over 50 staff, including a chef, catering manageress, cooks, washers-up and preparation hands. Things did not always run smoothly in the days before strict hygiene and food controls, but quality improved as menus were simplified.

People enjoyed the sociability of café bars, a respectable place for women in particular to meet over a cup of tea. During the war, they became even more popular, because customers could buy a hot meal without using ration coupons.

Once war broke out, these café bars became even more popular because customers could pay with cash, meaning ration coupons did not have to be used to buy meals. By 1941, they had been extended to a further 30 stores and by 1942, 80 stores had such facilities. From a business point of view, café bars were also useful because they filled the shop-floor gaps caused by wartime shortages of goods. The experience of catering on a mass scale was invaluable when Marks & Spencer opened 'communal kitchens' to help with the war effort (see page 182). The popularity of café bars continued after the War, with 107 in operation by 1948. They had a reputation for high standards of hygiene and cleanliness, with staff trained in food-handling, preparation and service.

However, post-war, their popularity declined and the last two surviving café bars, Leeds and Exeter, were closed in 1961. In 1986, a customer restaurant was opened at the MetroCentre in Gateshead, but it was not until 1997 in the Leeds branch that the M&S cafes were reintroduced, first as The Coffee Bar, later as Cafe Revive and now as M&S Cafes. The latter sell only Fairtrade organic coffee, part of the company's commitment to Plan A. There are now a variety of catering outlets on offer within M&S stores, ranging from Deli bars and Hot Food To Go counters to fully serviced restaurants and M&S Kitchens. The latter uses the best and freshest M&S ingredients in traditional dishes, with menus that change to reflect local and seasonal produce.

Today Marks & Spencer stores offer a range of in-house catering experiences from M&S Cafes to Deli Bars, Hot Food To Go counters and fully serviced restaurants. In 2004, Marks & Spencer committed to only selling Fairtrade coffee and tea in its M&S Cafes, followed by Fairtrade chocolate in 2006. This is part of the company's commitment to Plan A.

RAISE YOUR GLASS

Above: *When Marks & Spencer first started selling wine in 1973, it had only two varieties on offer: French Red Wine and French White Wine. The 'Chill before serving' notice was a helpful hint to less knowledgeable customers.*

In November 1973, a wine department was launched in 12 M&S stores. The initial range was tiny by today's standards: eight wines, four sherries and a small range of traditional beers. By 1974, this range had extended in size and was available in more stores. There were now 18 wines, plus sherry, vermouth, beers and cider. Liebfraumilch was particularly popular at 95p per bottle. Interestingly, the wines could not be labelled under the St Michael trademark, because this was already owned by a small wine company. Instead all alcoholic products were labelled Marks & Spencer.

Wine was a popular buy with the public. By 1983, there were nearly 50 wines on offer and by 1990, M&S was winning more medals than any other supermarket or off-licence in the *Sunday Express Magazine* wine awards. 'New World' ranges were launched in 1991, quickly becoming a favourite choice.

M&S continues to scoop top wine awards. In autumn 2008, it was nominated Supermarket of the Year at the Decanter awards, and Wine Merchant of the Year at the International Wine Challenge (IWC), the first retailer to win both. The online wine shop also goes from strength to strength, with about 550 wines currently on offer.

"In the early 1970s, I was working as an M&S merchandiser in Ladies' Knitted Tops. Meanwhile, I had developed an interest in wine and entered a wine competition in the Evening Standard *– which I won. News of this evidently percolated up to the Food division on the 6th floor and I was summoned to see Henry Lewis, Managing Director of Foods. He said, 'I hear you know a bit about wine? In that case, you can join the wine department which we have just set up.' At that time, M&S offered a very limited selection of wine, so it was a fantastic opportunity. It seems funny to think that is how things operated in those days – all rather ad hoc. My children have often suggested that if I had won a driving competition, I would have become the chauffeur."*

SIR STUART ROSE, CHAIRMAN

PAT
ON THE
BACK

As well as winning awards for its wine, M&S also scoops foodie achievements on a regular basis, including those organised by many of the regional agricultural shows. However, it is most proud of the recognition it receives for continually raising animal, poultry and fish welfare standards. In 1996, it established a Chair of Farm Animal Health, Food Science and Food Safety at Cambridge University with some of its suppliers, asserting its belief that it is ethically and morally right to treat food animals with care and compassion.

In 2002, Marks & Spencer was awarded Compassionate Supermarket of the Year by Compassion in World Farming (CIWF), following the organisation's most comprehensive audit of British supermarkets and their ethical practices. In 2006, it was named the number one retailer for sustainable fish in the Marine Conservation Society's (MCS) league table. In the same year, M&S invested in a lobster hatchery in Cornwall, helping to reverse dwindling lobster stocks and supporting the local economy. Also in 2006, it launched its exclusive Lochmuir salmon, the fish equivalent of the welfare-priority Oakham chicken range. This resulted in M&S becoming the first retailer to receive RSPCA Freedom Food approval across its entire salmon range in 2008.

In 2007, Marks & Spencer became the first UK retailer to stop selling imported white veal and calves' liver. It had banned the sale of 'crate-reared' veal back in 1995. Since January 2008, it has only sold high-welfare UK rose veal, which has the backing of Compassion in World Farming and the RSPCA.

All of this has resulted in praise and support from leading animal welfare groups. At the RSPCA Good Business Awards of 2008, Marks & Spencer was nominated Supermarket of the Year, praised particularly for its commitment to ensuring the welfare credentials of pork.

FREE RANGE RULES

M&S's commitment to promoting free-range eggs began in 1997 when it committed to selling only free-range. Since 2002, only free-range eggs have been used in M&S products, from the pastry in the pies to the glaze on sausage rolls — about 250 million eggs each year. In addition, the store sells a further 45 million free-range eggs annually. 2007 saw the launch of both free-range goose and duck eggs. In the same year M&S was awarded a Compassion in World Farming 'Good Egg' award.

"My wife Susie is a superb cook. However, she often doesn't have time to prepare a meal, and that is when we find M&S an excellent rescue service."

SIR STIRLING MOSS, RACING LEGEND

Right: *A happy hen lays the seal of approval on Marks & Spencer's commitment to selling only free-range eggs in 1997. In 2002, M&S introduced a policy of using only free-range in all of its food products.*

HAPPY
AND …

Of course everyone has their own favourite food at M&S, be it something classic and comforting like fisherman's pie or something sinful and indulgent such as walnut whips. Spring 1992 was a turning point in the company's food policy because it was the first time speciality luxury foods went on sale, at first solely at Marble Arch. These included caviar and dressed lobster. That autumn saw the launch of the first delicatessen counters, with the motto 'straight from our kitchen into yours'. The following year, the first in-store butcher's shop was opened in Camberley, extended to 17 more stores by the end of the following year. In 1995, wet fish counters were trialled at Marble Arch and Bromley. The latter also saw the first in-store bakery open in 1996.

The fact is that Marks & Spencer has long striven to ensure that the experience of shopping for food at its stores should not resemble the usual supermarket experience. By concentrating on blue-chip quality, ethical food production, luxurious ranges and downright delicious goods, it has found a very special place in all our hearts … and stomachs.

PERCY PIG

In October 2007, M&S announced it had sold the billionth Percy Pig since Percy was launched in 1993 – that's two Percy Pigs every second. Percy is the most popular pig on networking website Facebook, which hosts the Percy Pig Appreciation Society. This currently has over 21,000 members and debates such matters as how best to eat a Percy (ears first, apparently). You can also find advice on making a Percy Pig sandwich, freezing Percy and then sucking him until he defrosts, or demonstrations of two people eating a Percy at the same time. Strangely, walnut whip enthusiasts are far more secretive. Figures show that all ages and both sexes indulge in this retro treat, yet when a poll was taken asking people if they knew anyone who ate walnut whips, most people said no.

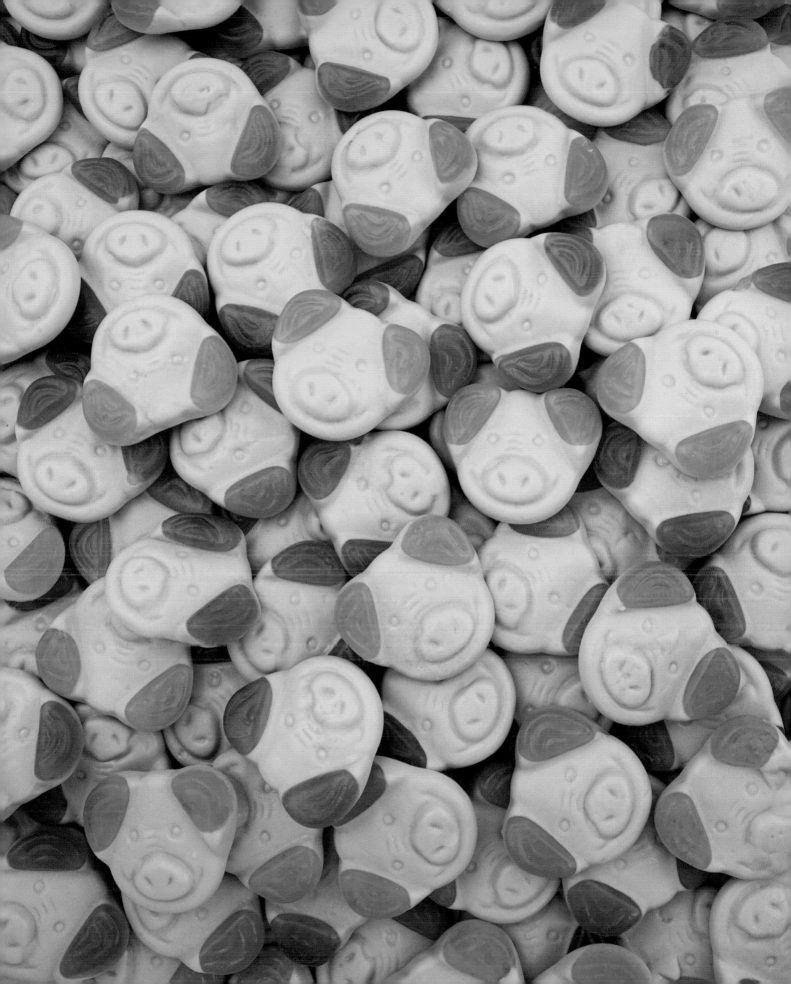

THIS IS NOT JUST …

"Working in the Marketing department during the launch of the 'Not Just Food' ads was memorable — and not least because of the huge and instantaneous response from customers. Then we started to receive text messages from friends directing us to websites such as YouTube where we discovered hundreds of 'M&S Food Porn' spoofs. Most of these couldn't be viewed from our offices because the M&S internet content filters automatically screen out unsuitable material. Some of them were executed to a very high standard, although I don't think the creative interpretation of 'This Is Not Just a Banana' would ever have passed the TV censor."

SUSAN AUBREY-COUND, EXECUTIVE ASSISTANT TO SIR STUART ROSE

A FEW OF OUR FAVOURITE THINGS

"The return home of Granny 'B' from a visit to M&S heralds a stampede amongst the junior Bothams and Grandad Beefy. Who gets to the garlic sausage first?! Without the M&S food halls, life would be very dull, although my waistline might be a little thinner!"

SIR IAN BOTHAM, SPORTSMAN AND CHARITY FUND-RAISER

"If ever I want to cook that special meal when guests come round, I know I can go to M&S and find the perfect items from starters right through to wine and after-dinner chocolates."

JEFF SMITH, MANCHESTER

"Walnut whips — from my first day of putting them on the shelves back in 1976."

CHRISSY GLADDLE, MELTON MOWBRAY

"It's got to be that chocolate pudding, the one advertised with Dervla Kirwan's seductive commentary."

NICHOLAS BATEY, EPSOM

A selection of the nation's favourite M&S food moments: Lochmuir smoked salmon (top left), a Gastropub lamb shank (top right), seafood platter of prawns, mussels and lobster (above) and celebratory champagne (right).

...HEALTHY

The M&S Turkish Delight is uniquely free of all artificial colourings and flavourings. In 2008, M&S successfully created a replacement formula for pink colouring using only natural fruit and vegetable extracts, including hibiscus and apple.

Back in 1972, *St Michael News* carried the headline, 'Marks & Spencer speaks out against artificial foods'. It reported that suggestions from suppliers to M&S concerning the manufacture of 'artificial foods', in particular proteins, had fallen on deaf ears. The company had made its opposition known to foods it perceived as smacking of chemicals and science.

Over the last few years, M&S has showed its commitment to 'real' food in many ways. Organic ranges were first introduced as long ago as 1989, but lack of availability and lack of demand meant they were withdrawn in 1993. In 2000, it tried again – first through a modest selection of organic fruit and vegetables, then through recipe dishes, sandwiches and prepared salads. It has also championed Fairtrade foods, switching its entire tea and coffee business to Fairtrade in 2006, as well as using only Fairtrade sugar in its conserves and marmalades. Fairtrade chocolate, fruit and wine is also available in store, as are Fairtrade cotton garments.

In addition, Marks & Spencer has taken steps to promote good health among its customers. In 2004, it led the way on salt reduction, reducing the salt content

of over 800 products. In 2005, it introduced the Eat Well logo, making it easier for customers to eat a healthy, balanced diet. It has also trained 1500 Healthy Eating Advisors, in collaboration with the British Nutrition Foundation.

Chemicals have been in the firing line too. GM foods were banned in 1999. By mid 2006, the company had also removed hydrogenated fats from all foods. In 2008, it became the first retailer to remove all artificial colours and flavourings throughout its entire food and soft drink lines.

In 2008, Marks & Spencer announced it had reached its target of banning ten more pesticides, these in addition to the 60 the company had already eliminated since 2002. A further nine will be banned this year (2009). This move supports its commitment to Plan A, which aims to use the most sustainable sources of raw materials with the least impact on the environment.

Our ready meals lack a certain something. Hydrogenated fats.

We've removed all the hydrogenated fats from our ready meals and are working to do the same to all our food. The finest ingredients, delicious sauces and a pinch of seasoning are the only things on the menu when it comes to preparing our Cook! Ready Meals. They are also 100% additive free. And without affecting the taste, all our ready meals and Children's Eat Well range are also free from artificial colours, flavouring and flavour enhancers. With our clear labelling policy, you'll always know what you're eating and what you're not. www.marksandspencer.com

YOUR M&S
look behind the label

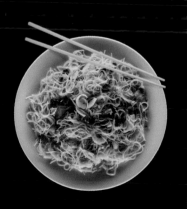

The 'Look Behind the Label' campaign, which drew attention to the fact that Marks & Spencer had removed hydrogenated fats from its foods by 2006. Since then, it has also removed all artificial colourings and flavourings.

WAR YEARS

During the Second World War, Marks & Spencer went shoulder-to-shoulder with the nation in trying to 'Keep Calm and Carry On' when presented with the many challenges of the day. Not only did it have its business to run and customers to keep happy – even with key goods, such as clothing and food in increasingly short supply – but it had its staff to care for, both those at home and those in the services. In addition, it had to contend with enemy bombardment, which damaged over 100 of its stores and resulted in the total destruction of sixteen, with tragic loss of life in consequence.

What is heartening about the war experience of Marks & Spencer is that it reflects the stoic, understated resilience and bravery of unsung men and women trying to preserve ordinary life in extraordinary circumstances that typified Britain during this period. Its staff 'did their bit' in every sense of the phrase and the company was proud to support them in every way possible. In this, it went beyond what was strictly required, for example by subsidising the service pay of its employees to bring it in line with pre-war salaries.

The M&S war effort was equally impressive, from raising money to present the nation with a Spitfire to rolling out subsidised canteens to feed those bombed out of their homes. These were traumatic and tumultuous years, but ones that ultimately strengthened the company when peace was declared.

M&S
GOES
TO WAR

Below: *The outbreak of war on Sunday 3 September 1939, as recorded in the diary of Mr Rogers, who worked in the Eltham store. The handwritten figures record the daily takings for provisions.*

Opposite: *Customers queuing at the temporary M&S store in a disused cinema at Sheffield the Moor in 1941. The original store was destroyed by bombing in early December 1940. The temporary store remained in use until 1952.*

Opposite below: *Company badges for ARP (Air-Raid Precautions) wardens and fire-watching personnel.*

When Simon Marks, Chairman of Marks & Spencer, addressed the AGM on 9 May 1939, war was uppermost on everyone's minds. As well as relaying the cheerful news that profits were up, Simon spoke of the seriousness of the international situation and detailed the company's preparation 'to safeguard the lives of workers and the public while on our premises' in the event of a war. A full-time air-raid precautions officer, Ralph Salaman, had already been engaged and 25 per cent of the staff had been trained in first aid or anti-gas precautions. An expenditure of £20,000 had already been incurred in taking these measures. When he also announced that members of staff were encouraged to join the Territorial Army with 'the necessary time off for training and to attend camp with full pay', there was applause from shareholders.

On Sunday 3 September 1939, Britain did indeed declare war against Germany. However, the impact of being at war was by no means instant. Britain entered the phase known as the 'Phoney War', which was shattered in the spring of 1940 when Nazi Germany invaded Holland, Belgium and Luxembourg before smashing its way through northern France towards the English channel at Abbeville, forcing the British Expeditionary Force to evacuate to Dunkirk. Over 330,000 troops were evacuated from the beaches, eventually reaching British shores. Marks & Spencer staff, trained in first aid, were among those on hand to give help where needed.

Earlier that year, Simon Marks wrote these words in the February issue of the *Staff Bulletin*:

"We are sending our recruits to the fighting services, already they number hundreds, as time goes on they will number thousands; and they include men in every one of our departments. We are staffing Air Raid Precaution services and providing for the safety of our own staff and customers in the event of an emergency. We are feeding evacuated children. We are training canteen workers. In many other ways we are playing our part, and the tale is not even half told. We can hold our heads high in these

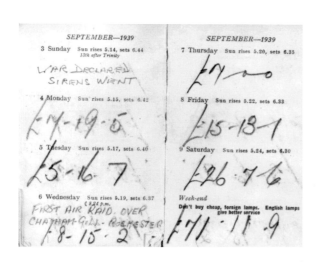

testing times, and say in time-honoured words: 'be strong and of good courage'."

By early 1941, supply ships were being sunk at the rate of over 20 per week by German submarines. Rationing was essential to the nation's survival, both to ensure a fair distribution of the essentials of life and to meet the production requirements of the armed forces. Food rationing was first introduced in January 1940, with different categories for adults, pregnant women and children.

The public were instructed to register for their rations with local tradespeople. Marks & Spencer food sections began to display notices saying 'Register here for cheese and preserves'. Meals bought at restaurants were not on ration, so the popularity of Marks & Spencer's own café bars grew as the war progressed. At many stores, the jostling of crowds impatiently waiting for the arrival of scarce supplies of food would accidentally pin staff against

Left: Three female staff in uniform: from left to right they are Kit Sharpe, Molly Jones and Elsie Marsh. Kit Sharpe donated this photograph to the archive. She worked in the Bognor Regis store, where she also met her husband.

the store wall. Occasionally, in a bid to keep impatient customers placated, merchandise would be sold straight from a lorry's tailboard.

During the war, Marks & Spencer became more than a distribution point for clothing and food. It was often the central focus not only of the staff who worked there – a place where troubles could be discussed with sympathetic colleagues – but also a place where the public could enjoy a similar respite from their troubles.

When a store was completely destroyed by enemy bombing, as 16 of them were, staff were often devastated by the emotional loss, even when deployed to other branches.

Right: This photograph from the archive of the Imperial War Museum shows one person's weekly food ration during 1941 and 1942. People could register at Marks & Spencer in order to receive certain rationed items.

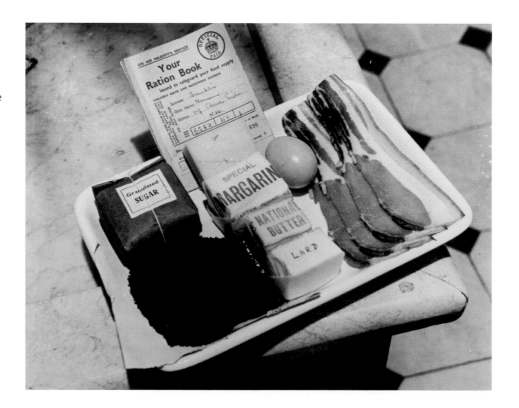

KINDERTRANSPORT

Kindertransport is the name given to the rescue mission that took place nine months prior to the outbreak of the Second World War, when the British government took in nearly 10,000 predominantly Jewish children from Nazi Germany and the occupied territories. The British Cabinet agreed to accept unaccompanied children ranging from infants to those aged seventeen. The majority of these children lost their families and homes for ever.

Simon Marks was among those who lobbied the government and who also sponsored some of the children. Incidentally, Simon knew that his name — and those of his family — were included in the Gestapo's Black List: those to be arrested following a successful invasion of Britain. In his desire to help Jewish children escape Nazi Germany, he was acting in a personal capacity — not as Marks & Spencer. It is likely that Israel Sieff was also among the lobbyists.

Among those who arrived at Liverpool Street, paid for by the Marks family, was Herbie Wolff, aged eight. He came with his sister, Lotte, having been put on the train at Frankfurt by his father and mother, who both knew they would never see their children again. Herbie had been dressed by his mother as a girl, in the hope that he would not be parted from his sister on arrival. It was a last gesture of maternal love.

But Herbie's association with M&S did not end there. He was later to work for over 30 years for the company, eventually managing stores in Catford, Gillingham and Walworth Road. Not only that, but his four sons all worked for M&S at some point, the eldest, Richard Wolff, notching up 36 years' service until he retired in 2007 as Director of International and Franchise. As Richard recalls: "For me, there was a certain emotional tie to M&S. If it hadn't been for families like the Marks and the Sieffs, my brothers and I would never have been born."

DEVASTATION

Opposite: *The Canterbury store was bombed during the night of 31 May–1 June 1942. This photograph shows how near it came to total destruction, but in fact it was the neighbouring properties on either side that suffered the most damage.*

In January 1942, a lone enemy bomber dropped a stick of bombs over the Lowestoft shopping centre, striking, among others, the Marks & Spencer store and tragically killing a sales assistant, Mrs Wright. It was the first of such casualties for the company.

An ARP (air-raid precautions) manual had been produced in July 1939 by Ralph Salaman with the aim of giving stores a procedure to follow in the event of an emergency. Because so many men were due for call-up, the chief ARP position was often filled by a woman. It was the ARP who was responsible for assembly arrangements after air-raid warnings and also the care of staff and customers during those raids. It was important, for example, to position people as far as possible from windows, skylights and entrances where they could be showered with lethal shattering glass.

The 1939 manual underwent many rewrites during the war as Ralph Salaman learnt bitter lessons from his meticulous inspection of the fire, bomb and shell damage inflicted on the company's stores. It was he too who organised 'The Chain Gang', a mutual aid system whereby Marks & Spencer, Woolworth's, British Home Stores, Boots and Lyons agreed to share staff canteens and rest rooms should any of their properties be damaged by enemy action. Under his guidance, a blast-proof shelter was built at every store and tin helmets were purchased in bulk to give additional protection to staff if required.

The obvious siting of shops such as Marks & Spencer in the centre of cities put them at grave peril from bombing. During the course of the war, about half of the Marks & Spencer stores and offices were damaged to some degree. Sixteen were destroyed completely and four in part. Eight members of staff were killed and 36 were injured while on duty. The casualty lists make sad reading, but in many ways it is remarkable they were so low – fortunately most raids took place at night when the stores were largely unoccupied.

The devastation of Coventry is well documented – one night of bombing which left 568 civilians dead, 863 seriously injured and the city in ruins. The staff manageress of Marks & Spencer, Miss MacPhee, made her way with typical staff loyalty to the site of the store in the early hours of the morning of 15 November 1940,

picking her way through burning rubble, to find: "... the inside of our building was reduced to approximately a twelve-foot height of fiercely glowing embers". Other destroyed stores included Harlesden, Castle Street, Bristol, Southampton, Sheffield, Swansea and Wallesey, where nightwatchman William Grisedale lost his life. Not long afterwards, Great Yarmouth and Birmingham (the largest Marks & Spencer store) suffered the same fate. Plymouth suffered five ferocious night attacks which devastated the city in April 1941. The Prime Minister, Winston Churchill, visited the city on 2 May and was cast into gloom by what he saw, repeating the words, "I've never seen the like" (noted in the diary of John Colville, his private secretary). The elegant Marks & Spencer store there was completely destroyed and these poignant words recorded in the company records:

I was not on duty when the fire started on Friday night but went to the store at 9pm and found the watchmen who were on duty attacking numerous incendiaries which

On the night of 9 April 1941, the heart of Birmingham was devastated when over 237 enemy bombers rained hundreds of bombs on the city. The Marks & Spencer store was among many buildings reduced to a smouldering ruin. (Imperial War Museum)

had fallen around the premises and adjoining property. At 11pm I heard that my wife and children were killed but I could do nothing about it so I carried on with my work at Marks & Spencer.
Fire Watcher's Report – Mr W. Stapleton

Tales of staff bravery were numerous, with many reported incidents of store staff dealing efficiently with incendiary bombs – these included Mr Mallet and Mr Shrewsbury who smothered two bombs on the roof of Head Office.

Exeter and Weston-super-Mare joined the list of destroyed stores, but it was Eastbourne that was to suffer not only the loss of property, but of life. The shopping centre was bombed on 18 December 1942, the last Friday before Christmas. The rubble of what had been Marks & Spencer included thirteen dead, twelve of them customers and one a member of staff, Mrs Florence Selway, senior floor-walker, who was killed while trying to shepherd customers to safety.

The Plymouth store was destroyed during the second of five ferocious nights of attacks that devastated the city during the last week of April 1941. During that time, 30,000 of its citizens were made homeless and 750 were killed.

SPIES

During the Second World War, the Head Office at Michael House, Baker Street, lost an entire floor, the 5th, for use by the Special Operations Executive (SOE). Even today many of the activities of this highly secret organisation are unknown, but it was set up in the aftermath of the 1940 evacuation from Dunkirk to help beleaguered Britain strike back against occupied Europe. The Germans referred to it as 'gangster school', while Winston Churchill famously declared its purpose was 'to set Europe ablaze'.

It is thought that the 5th floor housed the code or cypher section of the SOE. It was literally cut off from the rest of the building by a solid brick wall, which was routinely tested for its effectiveness by security men tapping it with hammers. Company staff continued to enter the offices by the main Baker Street entrance, while SOE personnel had their own entrance at the rear in Kenrick Place. Marks & Spencer staff were told not to converse with the unknown faces of the 5th floor: 'Good morning' or 'Good day' were the only permitted phrases.

The SOE occupied Michael House until 1946, a year after war ended. Its departure was marked by a bonfire of documents on the roof, which got so out of hand that the fire brigade were called. In fact it nearly achieved what enemy bombardment had not: the destruction of Head Office.

Left: *A V-1 exploded without warning just in front of the Lewisham store at 9.15am on 28 July 1944 – five staff lost their lives and a further 20 were injured. The total casualties amounted to a horrifying 56 deaths and 299 injured.*

Below: *These melted coins were all that remained of the cash float from one of the Marks & Spencer tills after the devastating raid on Bristol of 24 November 1940.*

Only one member of staff was uninjured following the raid.

However, it was 1944 that was to prove most devastating for the company. Clacton branch was destroyed by bombs dropped from aircraft in February of that year. Then in July, two of the London stores, Forest Gate and Lewisham, were destroyed by a new and terrifying form of aerial warfare: flying bombs or V-1s, which were ultimately responsible for the deaths of 6000 civilians.

Lewisham was particularly tragic in its consequences. At 9.42am on 28 July 1944, the V-1 broke through the overcast sky above Lewisham town centre, unheralded by sirens. The manager of the Marks & Spencer store, Sydney Spurling, was reading the morning's mail in his office. Nearby, in the General Office, was Mrs Clarke, an invoice clerk who was heavily pregnant. Other staff that day included Mrs Clamp, emergency management reserve, sales assistant Doris Taylor and 15-year old Alice May Thompson, a sales assistant who was helping the window-dresser complete a new display. When the bomb hit the store directly, all five were killed. A further 20 staff were injured. The total casualties of the Lewisham bomb were 56 dead and 299 injured. To Miss Hall, the staff manageress, fell the sad duty of comforting bereaved families, visiting the injured in hospital and identifying the five bodies in the mortuary. As she later wrote: "Personally I don't mind if I never have to go to a hospital for the rest of my life. As a matter of interest, my hair turned grey overnight – something I did not believe could happen – but I can assure you it did."

179

WOMEN
& WAR

Below: *Female staff fire-watching on the roof of the Exeter store before it was destroyed in May 1942. The woman on the far left was Mrs Mary Spike who donated this photograph to the archive.*

One of the greatest challenges that Marks & Spencer faced during the war years was a shortage of trained and skilled staff, because so many left the company's employ to enlist in the armed forces or civilian defence services. In September 1939, the number employed within the company totalled 20,700, but by June 1941 this had fallen to under 15,000 and by mid 1943 it was just 11,000. There was an even heavier decline among managers. At the outset of war, there were 463 male trainee managers; less than four years later there were just seventeen. Of the 2000 men employed by the company at the beginning of the war, over 1500 were in the forces when hostilities ended. This included two directors and all the directors' sons of military age.

The answer to such a severe staffing crisis was, naturally, to promote women from staff to management. This subject was discussed at a store managers' meeting held in Glasgow in May 1940, addressed by Frank Ross: "Already we have fifty potential manageresses and 120 girls have been nominated as potential first men (assistant managers)." It was advised that suitable staff should be given special training in Staff Management, Stockroom, Office and Store Management. The meeting concluded: "During this special training, female trainees should be treated by the manager as first man, ie, she should line up with the other men and go through the mail, discuss with them the store policy and generally receive personal attention from the manager."

Women replaced men, and girls replaced women, during the course of the war as over 1000 employees joined various war services, such as the Women's Armed Forces, nursing, transport, the Land Army, munitions production and other essential activities. Within the company, women were now engaged at

virtually every level – bar director – from divisional superintendent to sales assistant. The latter was arguably the most important job of all, as it meant coping on a day-to-day basis with bombing, rationing, shortages, anxiety for loved ones serving in the forces, and all the other many and varied difficulties of wartime life. It was the loyalty and determination of the female sales staff, submerging their personal worries to carry on with their work, that allowed Marks & Spencer to survive at all. As Simon Marks said in his tribute of 1941: "To our staff we owe far more than our customary tribute of appreciation. They have never failed to render loyal and devoted cooperation in the normal conduct of our enterprise and whenever the call has come, their courage in the face of great personal danger has been of the highest order. On repeated occasions, they have saved our stores from destruction. On behalf of you all, and on behalf of the Board, I express our profound gratitude to them."

WAR
EFFORT

There were many ways in which company staff assisted the war effort, including the knitting of innumerable garments by members of store staff. Indeed within two months of the outbreak of war, the company's Lancashire Division had completed 130 pairs of bed socks, 25 pairs of mittens, 34 pairs of operation stockings, two scarves and six balaclava helmets. Stores were told to make food for staff as appetising as possible so that nothing was wasted. The September 1940 issue of *Staff Management News* stated that: "Food is precious; to have it spoilt in preparation is a form of sabotage and must not be tolerated by anyone whose job it is to do battle on the Kitchen Front."

As the war progressed, stores held social events for servicemen, served wounded men for free in the staff canteen and organised theatrical entertainments. About 500 staff also worked as volunteers at the Royal Ordnance factory in Radway Green. Members of staff were also encouraged to join the Territorial Army. In addition, there was an army of staff who temporarily left the company's employ to take up essential production work in armament factories, the Land Army, the ARP, special police units and other vital organisations. Simon Marks's own wartime contribution was as Deputy Chairman of the British Overseas Airways Corporation (BOAC) – the nationalised forerunner of BA – an appointment which he held until January 1946. His business abilities there proved invaluable and were recognised by a knighthood in the summer of 1944.

Head Office staff raised enough money to donate an ambulance to the nation and, early in 1941, a staff collection raised the huge sum of £5000 – enough to purchase a Spitfire fighter aircraft (see page 184).

Flora Solomon, head of the Welfare Department, made her contribution to the war effort on a national scale. With a team of similarly able women in her department, she took the principle of staff canteens onto the national canvas during the war. An old community centre in Delgado Gardens, Kensington, was converted into a communal kitchen with catering equipment 'borrowed' from Marks & Spencer. Here people could buy a two-course hot lunch for 8d and tea at 1 1/2d per cup. Delgado Gardens was bombed in 1940, but the idea for such restaurants caught on. Later named British Restaurants, they were set up elsewhere in London

The British Restaurant where a two-course meal could be purchased for a shilling or less. It was Flora Solomon, head of Marks & Spencer Welfare Services, who established the concept, based on the subsidised canteen meals provided by M&S.
(Imperial War Museum)

and around the country. Customers were mainly the local bombed-out population, evacuees and children of working mothers.

Once a restaurant had been established and was running efficiently, it would be handed to the supervision of the local authority. Three mobile canteens, catering for old-age pensioners, were provided and serviced by the Welfare Department. Company personnel also assisted in the running of American Red Cross Clubs when the first US troops arrived in Britain in 1942. In towns and cities that were heavily blitzed, the Welfare Department and local store staff helped feed emergency workers, provide clothes for the homeless and feed the staff of neighbouring businesses damaged by bombing. The company even devised a thick, nourishing soup, known as Blitz Broth, for use in such situations.

THE MARKSMAN

Early in 1941, a staff collection raised the astonishing amount of £5000 for the presentation to the nation of a Spitfire fighter aircraft. A Mark Vb, serial no W3215, it was aptly named The Marksman. On 1st June, it was flown to the famous fighter station at Biggin Hill, Kent to join 'B' flight of no 609 (West Riding) squadron. From here on 22 June it enjoyed its most spectacular success while being flown by Sergeant Tommy Rigler.

Flying at 20,000 feet, east of Dunkirk, one of 609 Squadron's flight commanders spotted nine enemy fighters flying down the coast and shot one down in flames. Tommy Rigler downed three of the enemy fighters, an achievement that was noted both in The Times and on the radio. At one point he was hit in the wing by fire from one of the enemy aircraft and had to take evasive action. "Rigler, if you ever get out of this, you need never fly again," was what he later recalled saying to himself. Happily, he survived not only that particular escapade, but the war, retiring as Squadron Leader, DFC, DFM.

Sadly, The Marksman was shot down over northern France on 24 March 1942. The pilot, a 21-year-old Canadian called John Sills, did not survive. He is interred in the Pihen-les-Guines cemetery near Calais.

Left: *Squadron Leader Tommy Rigler, who in 1941, as pilot of The Marksman, shot down in one action three enemy aircraft.* **Below:** *The Marksman, purchased for the nation with £5000 donated by Marks & Spencer staff. (Imperial War Museum)*

ON ACTIVE SERVICE

By the end of the war, 1500 of the 2000 men employed by Marks & Spencer were serving in the armed forces. By 1945, 96 had died and 59 had become prisoners-of-war. Decorations or 'Mentions in Despatches' awarded to company staff totalled 124, including many of the most distinguished medals.

The Personnel Department individually wrote to men and women stationed around the world and to those in prisoner-of-war camps. Service pay was also subsidised by the company to bring it in line with the employee's pre-war civilian salary. These subsidies totalled £650,000 by the end of the war. The Welfare Department was also a source of practical help and comfort to the many families divided by wartime.

In January 1944, the first edition of the *Forces Bulletin*, a notebook size account of Marks & Spencer's activities, was distributed to the company's staff in the forces (see page 188). It brought M&S people together in the most unlikely places. How else could two infantrymen find themselves discussing the subtleties of Checking List complications when sheltering from a German counter-attack in a Normandy cowshed two days after the D-Day landings, as they later described when safely back home? All in all, 24 issues of the *Forces Bulletin* were printed, the last in June 1946.

However, the company also had a job to do in rehabilitating returning service men and women after the war. Where possible, the wishes of returning personnel were taken into full consideration regarding location or the type of job. Returning store managers were often posted first as 'guest' managers, working alongside the present incumbent (usually a woman) who would reintroduce them to the ways of the company. The Personnel Department saw itself as the 'shock absorber' between life in the forces and that of being a civilian once more.

For the company's women employees, it was inevitably the end of an era. Those who had so ably replaced men during the war years were once again demoted to assistant managers, staff manageresses, cashiers, departmental manageresses and head floor-walkers.

Left and below: *The bogus 'Marks & Spencers' laundry at Mersah Matruh, North Africa in 1943 – the 's' on 'Spencers' is of course a give-away. It was photographed by a member of Marks & Spencer personnel, who found himself posted there.*

FORCES BULLETIN

When Mr Frank Ross, editor of the Forces Bulletin, wrote his final leader in June 1946, his words were tinged both with sadness and pride:

"During the course of its career, the Bulletin has made many journeys to all parts of the world, to men serving on all battle fronts, and in many very remote places. It has travelled by air, land and sea, and has on occasions been dropped by parachute mail. It has been received by men in the front lines and on the home front. Our only regret was that we could not despatch it to the P-O-W Camps.

"It has been the means of many introductions between M&S men meeting in out-of-the-way places; it has gone the round of the camp and the messes; it has been read at home before being sent abroad; it has served the stores because of its general circulation, and to the staffs at store who despatched it, we are grateful for the many messages of good cheer and news of local interest which were included with it."

He did not exaggerate. The Forces Bulletin was a unique publication, which forged an unshakeable link between the company and its employees actively engaged in war. These are just a few of the tributes and experiences that its far-flung readers shared:

"To me, and many others, the Bulletin has afforded considerable pleasure during the years of exile, and its arrival was always eagerly awaited, bringing as it did, news of the Company, old colleagues and friends."
H. E. DOWEY

"At last I have some concrete news about my release. I shall be happy to be home once more and get settled to a more normal life . . . I get quite a kick out of going to Chinese restaurants and eating with chop-sticks, getting quite proficient at it now . . . One thing I am really looking forward to, is to get into bed without a mosquito net surrounding it."

MAJOR L.L. BEARMAN, RANGOON, BURMA

". . . all prisoners had to walk in the gutter to allow the 'Herrenvolk' to walk on the pavements . . . The Hitler Youth were very arrogant to the very end. They had been taught English well, ready for the time when they would rule England."

PRIVATE W.G. BROWN (captured in Tunisia)

And on coming back to civilian life again:

"One's first impression is that people show little sign of what they have been through, and, above all, retain a good sense of humour . . . Bus condructresses I should single out for the highest praise for their efficiency and tolerance under very trying conditions. I found it difficult though to get used to the idea of paying my fare, still imagining myself travelling in an Army truck."

MR L. STOFER

"The next thing which struck me was the high percentage of juveniles now employed in the store. To envisage a 15-year-old girl in charge of a counter was something foreign to my store experience; but I was favourably impressed by the competent manner in which some of these assistants were carrying out their duties."

MR E.F. OWEN

PEOPLE

Michael Marks understood the philosophy behind 'enlightened self-interest' even if he never came across the term. From the days of Penny Bazaars trading in markets, he did his best to keep staff comfortable and happy. His son, Simon, showed a commitment to the principle that was without precedent. Not only did he recruit the indomitable Flora Solomon to set up the first Welfare Department, but he ensured the company paid more than lip service to the idea by supporting every benefit she initiated, from subsidised canteens and chiropody to staff holidays and social events. Together he and Flora transformed the face of working Britain, leading the way for other companies to understand that staff welfare should be at the very heart of a business if that business is to prosper.

For one thing that both Michael and Simon Marks understood is that it is people who make businesses successful, who provide a human face to the goods you are selling. By taking care of their staff they enjoyed the benefit of staff who in turn took care of the company. Never was this more evident than in the years of the Second World War when Marks & Spencer survived in such good shape, thanks to the devotion and loyalty of its staff.

In 1962, the American writer S. J. Goldsmith made this observation:"If Britain is a welfare state, M&S is a welfare organisation within the welfare state. Their scores of thousands of employees used to be looked after well during their working days, in old age and in sickness long before the welfare state came into being . . . This way of running a business is known as 'Marks & Spencer economics'." It is a tribute to M&S that even after 125 years, staff speak of the company with such affection and refer repeatedly to the idea that they feel part of one big happy family.

CARING
FOR
STAFF

Right: *Mrs Flora Solomon, who established the Staff Welfare Scheme at Marks & Spencer in 1933. Under her guidance, this introduced everything from camping holidays and staff canteens to subsidised hairdressing and pensions.*

In America, Simon had seen first-hand that better working conditions made for more efficient, as well as happier, employees. But the trigger for a radical rethink about staff welfare was one comparatively trivial incident.

While visiting a store in the north of England in the early 1920s, Israel asked an assistant to pack something up for him. Simon glanced at the clock and said, "Don't start on that or you'll be late for your lunch." "Oh," she said, "that's all right, I won't be having any lunch." Israel asked her why not and she said she could not afford it. It transpired all the money she earned was needed at home. The two men were shocked by this reply and sat up late into the night formulating ideas that would help staff like her, those who were making sacrifices in order to help other family members. They decided the answer lay in providing a hot lunchtime meal at such a low cost that it would almost be uneconomical not to take advantage of it.

Then at a dinner party in 1932, Simon was castigated by his immediate neighbour, Mrs Flora Solomon, for the substandard conditions provided for staff. He was so impressed by her blunt approach that he recruited Mrs Solomon to take charge of the company's staff welfare. With his blessing, she went on to develop the finest such scheme in industrial Britain. Incidentally, her son, Peter Benenson, went on to found Amnesty International. Flora was born in Imperial Russia in 1895 and as Flora Benenson had made her way to England during the First World War, where she later married Colonel Harold Solomon. The Wall Street Crash disastrously affected her financial position, but as she later recalled, "I told myself I was in the same situation as everyone else and must try working for a living." When Simon made his offer she had virtually no business experience to speak of – but that in no way deterred her.

Under Flora's guidance, the Staff Welfare Service was formally established in 1933. This was a comprehensive system, including pensions, camping holidays, subsidised staff canteens, health service, dental service, subsidised hairdressing and staff rest rooms. Staff manageresses were appointed in every store, who were responsible for the welfare of shop-floor staff. The company dental service was such a success that it even won lavish praise in the *British Dental Journal* in 1960: "The success of this enlightened firm's voluntary action in dental health education

should be an example to the Minister of Health and his colleague the Minster of Education."

Subsidised staff canteens provided a midday meal consisting of meat or fish with two vegetables, bread and a sweet for sixpence. A cup of tea cost a further halfpenny and a piece of cake one penny. To put this into perspective, most sales assistant earned less than £2 (one pound then being equivalent to 240 pence) per week at this time, with store managers earning about £12 per week. Meanwhile, paid holiday entitlement was based on length of service, typically two weeks after a year's service.

By 1939, the company had also introduced various hospital and ophthalmic schemes as well as the dental one. The National Health Service would not be introduced for a further nine years, so this was on a private pay basis, heavily subsidised by the company's Welfare Department. The chiropody service was particularly recommended at the rate of a shilling per foot, foot hygiene being seen as essential for all sales assistants.

Flora was indefatigable in her championing of staff welfare. As late as 1962, she submitted one of her many reports to Simon Marks: 'A Report on Personnel, Welfare and Human Relations in the stores of Marks and Spencer'. Within this she shared with him her very human approach to caring for employees:

"*It may seem trivial to suggest resuming, for example, feminine customs like providing the birthday girl with a cake which she shares with her special friends during the tea break, or announcing on the notice board girls' engagements and congratulations on length of service, or presenting flowers on the eve of a girl's wedding; but such small attentions have a most improving effect on the general atmosphere. They are very pleasing to women and give them a sense of 'belonging'.*"

In the same report, she found staff canteens to be "splendid", continuing, "*I observed kitchens, equipment, menus and hygiene, all of which seemed to me to reach the highest standard. A good 90 per cent of the staff eat in the canteens, which confirms they are meeting a real demand.*"

When it came to social activities, she suggested "*The youngsters should be allowed to use record players in the luncheon breaks and even given facilities to 'twist' if they would like to . . . Here and there a staff manageress with imagination has improvised some odd corner for this, and the staff are delighted.*"

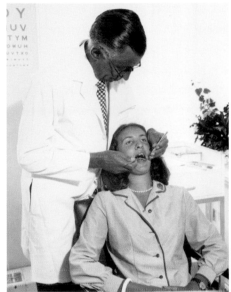

AT
WORK...

Opposite: *This 1947 recruitment leaflet, aimed at girls about to leave school, featured information on applying for a job with Marks & Spencer, including wages, sick pay, training, staff canteens and a full list of stores.*

In the early days of Marks & Spencer, Michael Marks recruited women to be managers rather than men, no doubt because they were cheaper. In 1909, a manageress was paid the relatively low wage of 15s per week plus commission on sales. However, the commission was quietly dropped and wages increased first to 30s and then by annual increments of five shillings. A Christmas bonus of £5 was also given. At the age of 15 or 16, recruited straight from school, sales assistants received between four and 18 shillings per week.

To be a shop assistant was a 'respectable' occupation for women in Edwardian times, while to be a warehouseman was to be in a position of trust. But while wages were low, hours were long – on Saturdays up to midnight. It was not until 1912 that a statutory half-day holiday was introduced. The manageress had a fortnight's holiday with pay and the assistants had a week. There was a 10-minute break

ETHICAL TRADING

Customers can trust that when they buy a product from M&S, the people making it are treated with respect, work in decent conditions without discrimination and earn fair rates of pay. The company demands this commitment from its suppliers, expecting them to continually raise standards and improve working conditions wherever in the world they are. In 1999, it was the first retailer to publish an Ethical Code of Conduct, called 'Global Sourcing Principles', outlining the standards expected for anyone trading with M&S. As a result of its commitment to ethical trading, M&S was voted top retailer by The Times *in 2008 when the newspaper ran a survey asking consumers, 'How well do you think retailers are doing at addressing social and environmental issues?'*

ESTHER BROWN

Esther Brown came to work for Michael Marks in 1893, one year before the beginning of the Marks & Spencer partnership. She was then 14 years old and she was hired as a mother's help to Hannah Marks. At first she worked on the market stall on Saturdays, but later she joined the Marks & Spencer staff full-time and graduated to the position of manageress at Oldham Street, Manchester, until she left in 1911. She emigrated to Australia but returned to Britain just before the Second World War. In 1964, M&S, hearing that she was seriously ill in Manchester, tracked her down and provided her with a pension and a flat. She died seven years later at the age of ninety-one.

in the morning and an hour for lunch. In 1909, the first staff training was introduced when the remarkable Miss Gibbs was given the title of 'travelling manageress', a role that gave her responsibility for the training of a number of assistants so they could be installed as manageresses as vacancies became available.

As Marks & Spencer expanded rapidly, management both increased and became more complex. In 1927, there were five women supervisors – a top tier of management. Specialised stocktakers reported to these supervisors and these too were often women, viewed by the board as being 'more adaptable than men'. However, in that same year there were more male managers in the company than manageresses, a trend that was to continue until the onset of the Second World War.

In 1934, a Personnel Department was created, headed by Flora Solomon. In an article she wrote for *Sparks* magazine under the title 'Management Without Tears', she asserted, "training for the job is an essential part of any welfare scheme". A training scheme was in fact introduced that year. All advertisements for staff had to go through the Personnel Department, with wages, conditions of work and training all considered as part of 'welfare'. A pension scheme was introduced a few years later for senior male management, as was the Marks and Spencer Benevolent Trust, which was endowed by Simon Marks and his family and Agnes Spencer, widow of Tom Spencer, and which was intended to provide retirement benefits for those outside the pension scheme. Another feature of M&S staff life was the 'long service' award, which recognised 25 or 40 years of service. This was a well-established practice by the 1950s and still continues today, with about 680 people celebrating these anniversaries in 2008.

Opposite: A scene from the Baker Street Head Office, probably from the early 1960s – while men took managerial positions, women were mainly allocated clerical work. **Above:** staff today enjoy friendly camaraderie.

...AND
AT
PLAY

Below: *Staff from the Sheffield the Moor store in the 1930s, playing tennis on the roof during their lunch break. This was the same store that was later destroyed in bombing during World War Two (see page 171).*

Flora Solomon's Welfare Department took great care to engender a sense of belonging among Marks & Spencer staff. Stores were reminded that birthdays should be noted, along with "the names of any Managers or men in training who excel in any branch of sport, giving details of their accomplishments or clubs for whom they have played". Staff dances were organised and some stores even had small libraries from which staff could borrow books.

Staff social activities included amateur dramatic societies, concerts, cricket matches, sports days and swimming galas. A staff sports club was opened in the 1930s, an outlet for the sports teams found in individual stores. Most popular were the holiday outings and trips abroad, which the Welfare Department also organised. However, these proved less popular in the post-war years and were eventually dropped in the late 1950s. Other social activities also waned.

Flora Solomon took the philosophical view that times had simply changed. In the report she produced for Simon Marks in 1962 (see page 194), she commented under the section entitled Social Activities: "*While I was on my visits I was often told that many of the social activities of the general staff have now ceased ...Though I used to be very enthusiastic about these activities, I have changed my mind about their relevance to present-day circumstances. Neighbourhood life has developed greatly. Workers much prefer to organise their own leisure ...The young want to be with boy friends, and the married women need all their spare time to deal with responsibilities at home.*"

Today many of the out-of-work activities that staff enjoy are related to fund-raising for charities, something the company wholeheartedly supports (see page 214).

Left: *Windsor store staff on holiday at Dymchurch holiday camp in Kent in 1936.*

Below left: *The Marspenza concert party performance in aid of the M&S Sports & Social Club for HM Forces, August 1941.*

Below: *Two happy Marks & Spencer campers.*

Right: Sam Worton, aka Cycling Sam, picked up his nickname during the five years he spent from 1950–1955 cycling to every Marks & Spencer in the country during his holidays and collecting autographs from all the store staff he visited.

CYCLING SAM

Could anyone have been a more devoted fan of Marks & Spencer than Cycling Sam? Sam Worton was a warehouseman in the Nottingham store, where he worked for over 32 years. He picked up his nickname when he decided to take a safari around every branch in the country on his bike, a journey that took all his holidays for five years, 1950 – 1955, and in which he visited 243 stores from Aberdeen to Truro and covered a distance of 7173 miles. At each store, he would ask all the staff present to sign his autograph book, now preserved in the safe hands of the M&S archive.

Recalling his endeavour in 1983, he said it was a chance conversation that inspired the idea:"I was cycling up to Glasgow from Nottingham to visit relatives and I thought I'd call into the Doncaster store for a cup of tea,"he explained."The manager there asked if I'd pass on his regards to the manager of the Carlisle store if I was passing and he, in turn, asked me to give his good wishes to the manager at Preston".

Sam's adventures were regularly covered by St Michael News *in the 1950s, which also printed beautifully illustrated maps of his route and excerpts from his diaries. When he arrived at his journey's end, the company headquarters in Baker Street at 12 noon on Monday 27 September, he was featured under the headline 'Alone He Did It'. Not that this was the end of the story for Sam. Once retired, he decided to revisit all the original stores on his route and see the ones that had opened in the meantime. Sam's second tour began in November 1980, but this time he was without his bike . . . instead he went by bus and train, taking advantage of day trip offers. Of course he noticed some changes, noting that the look of the stores had changed dramatically for the better, but also adding ruefully:"Of course in those days, everything was a lot cheaper."*

ALONE HE DID IT

Cycling Sam arriving at Head Office, Baker Street, his journey's end.

STIRLING 188

Good going Sam! may the second week of your journey be as interesting as your first.

All the best from Stirling staff.

W. Strachan
10/6/50

R. Cannon   Mr Joyce (cashier)
M. McMaster   D Wynne
B. Langlands   E. Elvin.
E. Lewis   M Young
B. Reid   a Drummond
                   G Brown (cook)

B. Lawton   14 OCT 1952

BARNSLEY 236

I'd rather paddle than pedal, but wish you all the best on your travels & trust you fulfil your ambition   E. H. Owen.

By. Murton S.M   V Hyde
Mrs Lumley.   G Glave
Mrs Firth   D. Fisher
Richardson   R Bostwick
Violet Cooper   S. Strutt
W W elford   J Paine.
M Halling   D. Hartley.
E. Barrowclough   B Machin
& Harris
K Lowe   M. Robertshaw
Baspinden   J Bowler
                      H Storey
                      J Fairweather
M. Wade.   Jno Moseley
                      H Moore.

IN AN ARTICLE entitled "Sam's Four Year Plan" which appeared in the June 1950 issue of "Sparks," we informed our readers that Sam Worton—Cycling Sam, the warehouseman from Nottingham—intended to visit every store in the business on his cycle, and that he hoped to achieve his plan during his annual holidays and occasionally on his weekly half-day. Since then we have given you from time to time some account of Sam's progress, but it is only now that we can tell you that it took Sam five years, and that he had arrived at his journey's end, Michael House, Baker Street, at twelve noon on Monday, 27th September as scheduled.

Sam, in all his travels, has been a stickler for being everywhere on time. That morning he had only travelled nineteen miles from St. Albans, the last leg of his tour, which in all had taken him 7,160 miles, up hill and down dale

in England, Wales, Scotland, as well as the Isle of Man.

In 1950 Sam's itinerary took him to Yorkshire, Northumberland, and Scotland and a few Lancashire Stores. The following year he concentrated on the Midlands, Wales, Devon and Cornwall and the South Coast. In 1952 he toured the home counties and the fringe of London. He had hoped to complete his plan in 1953, but in that year he managed to visit all our stores along the east coast from Hull to Southampton as well as a number of inland stores. By 1954 our Building Department had been so enterprising that new stores had been established once more at Swansea, Weston-Super-Mare, Bristol, Exeter and Plymouth, and thus Sam had to double back on his tracks to visit them. In June of this year too, he visited thirty-nine stores in the London area during one week, and he cleared up a few odd-

UNIFORM

Below: *Marks & Spencer staff around the year 1910. There was no uniform as such, but girls were expected to dress smartly.*

Right: *the back cover of the 1947 recruitment leaflet shown on page 197 – by this time a standard uniform had been introduced.*

In the early days of Marks & Spencer, there were no uniforms, but girls were expected to dress tidily and in dark clothes. Individual stores introduced uniforms over time, but there was not one shared by every store until around the time of the Second World War. Different ones were worn by those working in food. Over the years, uniforms were changed according to fashions, but one thing that is evident from those still retained in the M&S archive is that quality was high.

While female sales assistants were in uniform, male managers were expected to dress smartly in a suit and tie. Standards were exacting. Freda Graham, now retired, remembers beginning her M&S career as a Saturday girl in the Portobello Road store in 1970 when she was just fifteen: "When you came down the stairs onto the sales floor, there was a mirror at the bottom, with the words 'This is how the customer sees you'. The staff manageress was also there waiting to check:

* Only brown or black flat shoes.
* American tan tights.
* No garment showing under your uniform and length of uniform just below the knee.

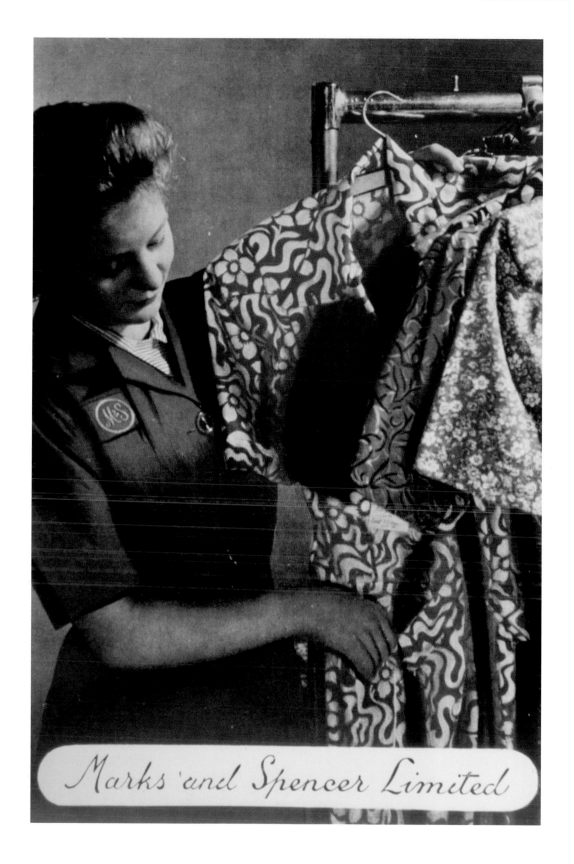

Below: M&S staff members in the 1950s.

Opposite: The photo (top) donated by Miss Dorothy Jackson shows the M&S uniform in the 1960s, as does the one on the right; the middle image dates from the 1980s, while the bottom one shows staff today.

* No large earrings or jewellery.

And she was ready with rubber bands if your hair came down to your shoulders, so you had to tie it back."

Jackie Harsley has a similar recollection: "When I started work for M&S in 1973, all the girls were lined up in front of a mirror to have our hemlines measured two inches above the knee because uniforms were a standard length. One of my shorter colleagues looked as though she was wearing an evening dress."

Today employee uniforms are being developed to reflect M&S's commitment to Plan A – with fleeces made from recycled plastic bottles – a polyester fleece identical in feel to virgin polyester.

MAGAZINES & BOOKS

Opposite: St Michael News *was the most enduring of the Marks & Spencer in-house publications. Dating from 1953 until 1999, it kept staff abreast of new products and developments. It then re-launched as* On Your Marks *and is now* Your M&S.

The establishment of the in-store publication, *St Michael News* in 1953, was designed both to forge even stronger links within the Marks & Spencer community and also to keep staff informed of products and developments. It was a lively house journal, which recruited professional journalists and went on to win awards for its coverage of events such as the Manchester bombing (see page 212). It continued until July 1999, metamorphosing into *On Your Marks*, which ran until May 2004, before changing to its present name of *Your M&S*.

However, it was by no means the first in-house publication. *The Marks & Spencer Annual*, which contained a variety of reading matter and was edited by Simon Marks, was published between 1909 and 1915. Internal publications included *Staff Management News* (1938–1940), the *Staff Bulletin* (1940–1949), *Forces Bulletin* (see page 188), which replaced the *Staff Bulletin* from 1944–1946, and the *Training News Bulletin* (1944–1947). The oldest was the *Weekly Bulletin* of 1927–1929, which was produced by Head Office for store managers and gave advice on best-selling products and how to promote certain lines for fastest profit. Other M&S publishing ventures included a juvenile Alphabet and Reading book, a Juvenile Magazine, a Mammoth Library and an omnibus version of popular classics.

In 1987, M&S also launched a publication for customers, *The M&S Magazine*, one of the first retailers to do so. Today called *Your M&S*, it boasts one of the largest circulations in Britain, well over four million readers per issue. Marks & Spencer also has the largest range of own-brand books in Europe, selling a book roughly every five seconds.

WEIDENFELD & NICOLSON

"At the end of 1947, Israel Sieff, then Vice-Chairman of Marks & Spencer, suggested to George Weidenfeld that he should produce a series of children's classics to be sold exclusively through the M&S stores. This was published under the name The Heirloom Library. George Weidenfeld and his partner, Nigel Nicolson who were then editing a literary magazine, Contact, *took advantage of this bonanza to turn themselves into a 'proper book-publishing outfit', so in 1948 they set up the publishing firm of Weidenfeld & Nicolson. The first publishing list appeared in 1949. What pleasing symmetry that we have produced this book together exactly sixty years later!"*

MICHAEL DOVER, PUBLISHER, WEIDENFELD & NICOLSON

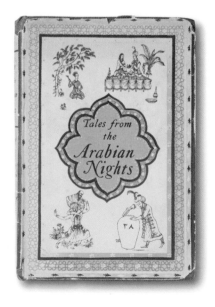
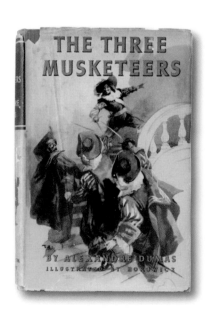

Left: *These beautifully illustrated children's classic stories were part of the Heirloom Library, a publishing venture begun by George Weidenfeld and Nigel Nicolson at the suggestion of Israel Sieff. They were sold exclusively through Marks & Spencer.*

Above: *In 1987, Marks & Spencer became one of the first retailers in Britain to launch a magazine specifically for its customers, which is today called Your M&S. It boasts a readership of over four million per issue – one of the largest in the publishing world.*

TERRORISM

The morning of Saturday, 15 June 1996, dawned bright and sunny in Manchester. However, by 10am, Margaret Jacques, deputy general manager of the M&S store, had been told by police they suspected a bomb had been planted in a van just outside the shop entrance. At once she and her staff began to evacuate customers to Victoria station. Once the store had been safely cleared, police planned to carry out a controlled explosion, but before they could do so the bomb went off – the biggest ever planted by the IRA on the mainland. Not only did it devastate the city centre, annihilating the Marks & Spencer store, but it also injured 226 people, although fortunately none were killed. As Margaret Jacques told *St Michael News* at the time: "It was so loud I can't describe it. I heard someone screaming and someone shouted to get down. Then there was silence and some glass from the station roof rained down on us. My most vivid memory is of getting up and seeing blood all over the ground. Then a man came running towards me saying he needed help."

The M&S first-aid team established a first-aid post, staying with the injured until they could be moved to hospital. One week after the bomb exploded, almost all the store's 571 staff were reunited in the city's Piccadilly Hotel where the then Chairman, Sir Richard Greenbury, praised their courageous response. It was an emotional meeting, with staff likening it to being a family without a home. Two replacement stores were opened less than five months after the bomb and Sir Richard promised the original store would be rebuilt 'better than ever'. On this, the company was true to its word, opening a new superstore on Market Street on 25 November 1999. As staff member Anne Sweetmore recalls: "I have lots of memories of my years at M&S, including the teamwork and support after the bomb. Everyone pulled together through tears and laughter . . . we also had a memorable 'comeback' party when the store reopened."

When London was targeted during 7/7 in 2005, the Edgware Road branch of M&S was directly affected. During the hours after the bombing, staff offered invaluable help to the emergency services, sheltering and treating the wounded, and providing both victims and emergency services personnel with food, drink and comfort where they could.

ASSASSINATION ATTEMPT

Joseph Edward Sieff — known as Teddy — was Israel Sieff's younger brother, who in turn became Chairman of Marks & Spencer between 1967 and 1972. Teddy Sieff is famous for surviving an assassination attempt by Carlos the Jackal (real name Ilich Ramirez Sanchez) who shot him through the mouth in December 1973, while he was in the bath at home in St John's Wood. The bullet hit Teddy in the face through his right upper lip and shattered his jaw bone on that side. Fortunately, Mrs Sieff had the foresight to turn him on his side to prevent him inhaling his own blood. What saved his life were his good teeth — doctors concluded that healthy canines slowed down the momentum of the bullet stopping it severing vital blood vessels to the brain. Carlos is thought to have been working for one of the Middle Eastern countries hostile to Israel. From that time, Marks & Spencer chairmen were viewed as terrorist targets by the security services. Sanchez was eventually captured in the Sudan in 1994 and was sentenced to life imprisonment in 1997.

The irony of the attack by the IRA in Manchester was that for many years, M&S was one of the only leading high street retailers to continue trading in Northern Ireland, as many staff remember:

"It was the only UK chain to remain fully committed to Belfast and Northern Ireland for many dark years during the 'troubles'. Many major companies steadfastly refused to invest in Northern Ireland during 30 years of conflict, but M&S not only remained open, but invested and expanded."

STEWART O'HARA, BELFAST

"M&S remained faithful to people throughout difficult times in northern Ireland. It provided jobs when others didn't."

GERALDINE MCCONVILLE, COUNTY ANTRIM

HERE TO HELP

From the very beginning of its history, Marks & Spencer has recognised the importance of giving back to the community, their customers, both at national and local level. Michael Marks himself was a notable philanthropist, who believed in sharing his good fortune with others. His son, Simon, continued this tradition – in 1963, the year before his death, the company donated £1.4 million to charitable causes. But it is not just about money. Marks & Spencer has an unshakeable belief at the core of its heritage that it is also important to invest time and skill when it comes to making a difference.

The best example of this in action is the Marks & Start work experience initiative, aimed at helping people who face significant barriers to getting into employment by giving them the chance to build up their skills and confidence in the workplace. The main groups targeted include disabled people, homeless people, lone parents wishing to return to work and the young unemployed. Each recruit is teamed with a 'buddy' who mentors them through the scheme and the company pays expenses, such as travel. Since 2004, over 2500 adults have benefited from these work placements, which are typically two to four weeks long, and of these around 1000 have gone on to gain employment either with Marks & Spencer or with other employers. Even more importantly, after six months 75 per cent are still in employment.

Marks & Start is the biggest company-led work experience programme in the

UK and Ireland, with 240 stores in partnership with a number of related charities, including DisabledGo, Business Action on Homelessness, One Parent Families/Gingerbread and The Prince's Trust. It is a success story of which the company is proud, but the true heroes are the 2000 in-store buddies who have committed so much of their time and energy to making it happen.

Many of the people who work at M&S devote a great deal of time and energy to raising funds for charities close to their hearts through a host of imagina-

Sir Stuart Rose congratulating the Aberdeen store team at the 2008 National Volunteer Awards. They were runners-up in the 'best fund-raising group for a corporate cause-related marketing charity'.

"My proudest moment was at the Awards ceremony in London in 2007 when I was runner-up for Service Person of the Year in Northern Ireland. It was like a night at the Oscars and I was the star."

GERALDINE MCCONVILLE, COUNTY ANTRIM

tive activities from marathon-running, fashion shows, cycle rides and race nights to balls, tombolas and afternoon teas. M&S has long recognised its employees' commitments to good causes and encourages great teamwork by matching the funds they raise up to £3000 when they work in a team of five or more. In 2007, the company supported around 1000 employees with £220,000 donated to about 80 charities.

The M&S Employee Volunteer Awards night is a chance for M&S to recognise, celebrate and reward its employees for their many achievements in supporting their local communities through volunteering and fund-raising, or by working on the Marks & Start work experience programme. In addition, there are also rewards for Plan A champions.

The company too does its bit. Each store has an annual budget which allows it to donate to local charities at its own discretion. At the other end of the scale is the support that M&S gives to its selected charities, notably Breakthrough Breast Cancer, Oxfam, Groundwork and WWF. Breakthrough Breast Cancer, for example, has launched the Breakthrough Generations Study, the most comprehensive study yet undertaken into the causes of breast cancer. The research will be funded by money raised through M&S and will involve more than 100,000 women over a period of 40 years.

THE
M&S
TIMELINE

For 48 years, Simon Marks dominated the fortunes of Marks & Spencer, but it would be wrong to give the impression that his is the only contribution that shaped the business it is today. When his friend Israel Sieff married Simon's sister Becky, and Simon in turn married Israel's sister Miriam, it cemented a union that saw many members of the Marks and Sieff families enter the business that Michael Marks had founded. Simon's younger sister, Miriam, married Harry Sacher, so the grandchildren of Michael included those by the name of Marks, Sieff and Sacher. These three families dominate the first one hundred years of the Marks & Spencer family tree.

However, it is the Chairmen of M&S who have had the greatest personal influence on its development. Since Simon Marks's death in 1964, each successive one has branded the company with his own vision of what the name Marks & Spencer means to its customers and what it should strive to achieve for its future.

1884	1894	1907

Michael Marks
1884–1907
Founder

Michael Marks
The first section of this book is dedicated to the life and hard work of Michael Marks and his wife, Hannah. A Jewish immigrant from Russian Poland, Michael began as a pedlar, built up a business founded on Penny Bazaar market stalls and eventually expanded this into a chain of nationwide shops. His 11-year partnership with Tom Spencer gave the company the name by which it is still known today. Father of Simon Marks, Michael was an ambitious but kindly man, who was remembered as a great philanthropist as well as an astute entrepreneur when he suffered his premature death in 1907.

Tom Spencer
Partner
1894–1905

William Chapman
1907–1916
Chairman
(as Executor to
Tom Spencer)

Israel Sieff
1964–1967
Chairman

Israel Lord Sieff

Simon Marks's friend, brother-in-law and long-term business colleague, Israel became Chairman following Simon's death. With Israel's help, Simon had wrestled back control of the company from William Chapman in 1916, and he remained Simon's loyal ally for the next 48 years. He was pivotal to the growth of Marks & Spencer, not least because he was the perfect foil to Simon's more acerbic manner. Indeed he has been described as 'the velvet glove around Simon's iron fist'. Israel was the more intellectual of the two, interested in foreign affairs and an eloquent communicator. His chief legacy was his attention to and care for the staff – he excelled at fostering human relationships. Under his chairmanship, Israel opened up the company to new ideas. His partnership with Simon was once described as 'two men who together were worth ten'.

Simon Marks
1916–1964
Chairman

Simon Marks, Lord Marks of Broughton

Rightly described as a retail revolutionary, Simon Marks transformed his father's affluent business into a giant of British retailing. Under his leadership, the company became an emblem of the high street, offering quality goods at affordable prices. His innovations fill this book, from the decision to deal direct with suppliers to his determination to sell only truly quality food. Mercurial, uncompromising and often downright frightening, he commanded the respect of his staff, if not always their affection. However underneath an intimidating exterior, he hid a warm heart, introducing a company welfare scheme that was the most comprehensive and committed of its type.

1916　　　　　　　　　　　　　**1964**　**1967**

Edward Sieff
1967–1972
Chairman

Joseph Edward (Teddy) Sieff

Israel's younger brother, Teddy Sieff, joined the company in 1933 and was first appointed to the board in 1939. Simon delegated much of the day-to-day running of the company to him during the war, because Simon himself was often absent owing to affairs of national importance and Israel was involved in the USA and Canada, developing a textile export business at the request of the Board of Trade. Teddy's particular talent was textiles and as a director he had formed the Merchandising Committee which coordinated the work of various textile departments. A capable, likeable and unassuming man, he is also notable for surviving the assassination attempt by Carlos the Jackal (see page 213).

**Derek Rayner
1984–1991
Chairman**

Sir Derek Rayner, later Lord Rayner of Crowborough
Derek was the first non-family member to become Chairman and was the protégé of Marcus Sieff. Having joined the business in 1953 at the age of 27, he had been a director for 17 years when he finally became Chairman. Cultured and brilliant, Rayner had by then also made a name for himself as a government adviser, first to Edward Heath and later to Margaret Thatcher. A passionate believer in expansion, he oversaw M&S acquiring out-of-town sites in the UK, as well as opening the first M&S store to open in South-East Asia, in Hong Kong. In 1988, M&S bought the Brooks Brothers menswear chain in the US, allowing a strong presence throughout the USA. Derek remained true to the traditional ethos of M&S, but also introduced new ideas at every level, from improved information systems and transport to modernisation of stores.

1972 **1984**

**Marcus Sieff
1972–1984
Chairman**

Marcus, later Lord Sieff of Brimpton
Israel Sieff's son, Marcus, joined the company his grandfather had founded in 1935. His personal domain was the food division and he is largely credited with M&S's expansion into truly quality foods. Under his chairmanship, M&S began serious international growth, first by acquiring a 55 per cent stake in the People's Department Stores, Canada; then in 1975, the first M&S store opened on the Boulevard Haussmann in Paris. A true leader who commanded respect and knew how to use his influence, Marcus had a vision for growth and saw the need to modernise. Charming and witty, he eventually stepped up to become President of M&S, travelling the world to lecture on the company's ethos.

**Richard Greenbury
1991–1999
Chairman**

**Richard Greenbury,
later Sir Richard**
Richard worked his way to the position of Chairman from the shop floor upwards. He joined Marks & Spencer in the early 1950s, straight from school, as a management trainee. By his early 20s, he was working as a departmental manager at 'The Arch', where he was singled out by Simon Marks and learnt much of the business by the great man's side. Imposing and forceful, Richard prided himself on being tough, fair and honest – but, like Simon, he never suffered fools gladly. As Chairman, he continued the expansionist policies of Derek Rayner, most particularly with edge-of-town stores and an increased presence abroad. By 1995, M&S had seven Hong Kong stores, 29 in Europe and franchised operations throughout much of Asia.

**Brian Baldock
1999–2000
Chairman**

1991   1999   2000

**Peter Salsbury
1999–2000
Chief Executive**

**Luc Vandevelde
2000–2004
Chairman**

Luc Vandevelde
Luc Vandevelde became Chairman of M&S as the company's profits were slumping. A cultured Belgian who spoke five languages, his business pedigree included top management roles at Kraft and chairmanship of the French supermarket group Promodes. Luc's appointment of George Davies and the creation of per una in 2001 marked a significant shift in the company's fortunes and by 2002 confidence was slowly beginning to return, although recovery was still some way off.

Philip Green

Sir Philip Green deserves special mention, because – like William Chapman nearly a century before – he was very nearly successful in seizing control of M&S from what many perceived to be its 'rightful' owners. Having withdrawn his earlier bid plan, by 2004 he was determined to take another crack at the company that has been described as 'the crown jewels' of the high street.

This was before Stuart Rose was invited to be Chief Executive of M&S, but he and Philip already knew each other personally: it was Stuart who, as Chief Executive of Arcadia (a high street fashion retailing business that included Top Shop, Burton and Dorothy Perkins) had sold that business to Philip, making him the most powerful force on the high street after M&S. At that point, the two men held each other in mutual respect and in fact Philip had privately included Stuart in his game plan for a M&S takeover. At this point M&S's profits were falling, a particularly bad sign when the rest of the country appeared to be in the grip of a consumer boom.

However, rumours that Philip was planning a takeover bid pushed the share price up, forcing him to make a statement of his intentions on 27th May: "Revival, a company owned by Philip Green and members of his family, confirms that Revival is considering a possible offer for Marks & Spencer ..." The news caused an immediate leap in the share price and 105 million shares were traded.

The very next day, the M&S board, led by Paul Myners, approached Stuart Rose to take over as CEO. Before the job offer was formally on the table, there was one final face-to-face meeting between Stuart and Philip. It was a combative conversation to say the least: "Philip can be quite intimidating when he wants to be," recalls Stuart, with typical understatement. On Monday 31 May, Stuart's appointment was formally announced by M&S. Philip interpreted Stuart's acceptance of his new role as a personal betrayal. His fury became clear on Friday of the same week when he accosted Stuart outside the M&S Baker Street offices to the astonishment of staff watching from their windows. To say things got personal between the two men barely scrapes the surface. This was a bitter fight between Philip, a pugnacious, self-made man who dislikes being thwarted and Stuart, a man who relishes a challenge.

At the 14 July 2004 AGM, held in London's Royal Festival Hall, Stuart faced M&S shareholders – some of whose families had held shares since the 1930s. It was abundantly clear from the meeting that there was overwhelming private shareholder support for the board against the approach from Revival, and it was their loyalty that apparently proved too much for Philip Green. After six weeks of manoeuvres and counter-manoeuvres, he pulled out of the fight that day – before ever making a formal bid for the company. After all the excitement and adrenaline, his complete withdrawal took everyone by surprise – including Stuart: "Everyone just sat there stunned. No one got the champagne out – everyone was just knackered."

However, as M&S recovered, so did the relationship between the two men. Today they maintain the healthy respect for each other they originally enjoyed. In fact it could be argued that the threat of a Philip Green takeover was the saving of M&S: it resulted in a clean sweep of a new broom, leading to the renewed health, vigour and energy that the company enjoys today.

2002

**Roger Holmes
2002–2004
Chief Executive**

**Paul Myners
2004–2006
Chairman**

Paul Myners, Lord Myners of Truro

Paul Myners became Chairman of M&S in 2004, having served as a non-executive director from 2002. His professional history includes both financial journalism with the *Daily Telegraph* and a banking career with N.M. Rothschild & Sons. In 1985, he was appointed Chief Executive at Gartmore, later acquired by the NatWest Group, of which Paul became a member of the board in 1997. He has also played a part in public life, most notably as an adviser to the Treasury. A renaissance man with many cultural interests as well as blue-chip City credentials, he was instrumental in the appointment of Stuart Rose as CEO in 2004.

Stuart Rose
2004–2008
Chief Executive;
2008–present
Chairman

Sir Stuart Rose
Stuart began his retail career in 1972 as a management trainee with Marks & Spencer under the chairmanship first of the Sieffs and then of Derek Rayner. By 1989, he was commercial director heading up the European division based in Paris. He was then recruited by the Burton Group (later Arcadia) as buying and merchandising director for Debenhams, rising to managing director of Evans and subsequently of Dorothy Perkins. In 1997, he became chief executive of Argos and a year later, of Booker. Stuart rejoined Arcadia Group plc as chief executive in 2000 and left in 2002, following its acquisition by Philip Green. Stuart became Chief Executive of M&S in 2004 and Chairman in 2008. Credited with bringing a lot of energy into the business, he is determined to bring M&S into the 21st century without sacrificing any of the traditional ethos of the business.

2004   **2006**   **2008**

Terry Burns
2006–2008
Chairman

Terry Burns
Lord Burns of Pitshanger

Terry Burns is a former Whitehall mandarin, who was a chief economic adviser to the first Thatcher government, rising to permanent secretary of the Treasury in 1991. After being awarded a life peerage in 1998, he then began a varied career in the private sector with non-executive directorships at Pearson, Legal & General and British Land. Before taking over as chairman of M&S, he was chairman of the Welsh water company, Glas Cymru, and of the Abbey National. Outside of the boardroom, his career has been no less impressive – he has been chairman of the National Lottery Commission and led the government review into fox-hunting. He is also Chairman of the Royal Academy of Music and a keen supporter of Queen's Park Rangers. His chairmanship at M&S was brief, but fruitful: it was Terry who invited Kate Bostock to become a member of the board.

ACKNOWLEDGEMENTS

Helen Chislett would like to to thank all those at M&S who made valuable time to help with the research for this book, in particular Sir Stuart Rose, Susan Aubrey-Cound and Sarah Edwards for driving the project through. A special thank you also to the M&S archivists, Kirsty Shields and Hollie Fisher, who were unflagging in their help and commitment. I am also indebted to the many M&S staff members, both past and present, who took time to talk to me; and also to some of the store's more famous fans for sharing their favourite M&S moments. A huge thank you to the other members of the editorial team, most particularly David Rowley for his inspired design and art direction, Michael Dover for steering the book so wisely, Debbie Woska for her patient editing and Lesley Davy for keeping us all on the straight and narrow. To John, Rosie and Flo, a huge and heartfelt thank you for all your love and support.

The M&S Archive: this book is largely built on research conducted at Marks & Spencer's own archive, which relocates in 2009 to the University of Leeds, the birthplace of the original Penny Bazaar at the market in Kirkgate. For the first time, members of the public will have access to the many fascinating artefacts and documents, 60,000 in total, that make up this unique resource.

BIBLIOGRAPHY:
Judi Bevan, *The Rise and Fall of Marks & Spencer And How It Rose Again*, 2007, Profile Books Ltd
Paul Bookbinder, *Simon Marks, Retail Revolutionary*, 1993, Weidenfeld & Nicolson Ltd
Paul Bookbinder, *Marks & Spencer, The War Years, 1939–1945*, 1989, Marks & Spencer plc
Asa Briggs, *Marks & Spencer, 1884–1984, A Centenary History*, 1984, Octopus Books Ltd
Nathan Goldenberg, *Thought For Food*, 1989, Food Trade Press Ltd
Robert Peston, *Who Runs Britain*, 2008 Hodder & Stoughton
Goronwy Rees, *St Michael, A History of Marks & Spencer*, 1969, Marks & Spencer Ltd
Rachel Worth, *Fashion for the People*, 2007, Berg

PICTURE CREDITS

First published in the United Kingdom in 2009 by Weidenfeld & Nicolson.
10 9 8 7 6 5 4 3 2 1

Text © Marks & Spencer plc 2009
Design and layout © Marks & Spencer plc 2009

A CIP catalogue record for this book is available from the British Library.

ISBN 978 0 297 85873 7

DESIGN AND ART DIRECTION BY David Rowley
EDITED BY Debbie Woska and David Atkinson
COLOUR REPRODUCTION BY DL Interactive UK
PRINTED BY Printer Trento Srl, Italy
BOUND BY L.E.G.O. SpA, Italy

Printed on GardaMatt Art by Cartiere del Garda, an ISO 14001 certified and EMAS registered company. Cartiere del Garda is particularly attentive to the choice of its suppliers and uses selected pulp coming from producers that implement good management practices in forestry resources.

Weidenfeld & Nicolson
The Orion Publishing Group
Orion House
5 Upper St Martin's Lane
London WC2H 9EA

An Hachette UK company.

Mixed Sources
Product group from well-managed forests and other controlled sources
www.fsc.org Cert no. CQ-COC-000012
© 1996 Forest Stewardship Council